PAYING THE PIPER

BRIAN MONTEITH

One of the Scottish Parliament's more colourful and contro-
versial members, Brian Monteith is used to swimming against
the prevailing tide in Scottish politics. After cutting his teeth
in student politics, he worked for Michael Forsyth, Teddy
Taylor and Iain Sproat. He ran campaigns against devolution
in 1979 and 1997 and was elected to Holyrood in 1999,
where he was Tory spokesman for education, culture and
sport, and then finance, before becoming an independent
member in 2006. He is convener of the Scottish Parliament's
powerful audit committee and a regular columnist in the
Scottish papers, commenting on economics, culture and
politics.

PAYING THE PIPER

From a Taxing Lament to a Rewarding Jig

Brian Monteith

BIRLINN

First published in 2007 by
Birlinn Limited
West Newington House
10 Newington Road
Edinburgh
EH9 1QS

www.birlinn.co.uk

ISBN13: 978 1 84158 587 1
ISBN10: 1 84158 587 4

British Library Cataloguing-in-Publication Data
A catalogue record for this book is available from the
British Library

Typeset by Textype, Cambridge
Printed and bound by Cox & Wyman Ltd, Reading

Dedicated to
Alfred Sherman, Ralph Harris and Frank Johnson,
all of whom were an inspiration to me in the '80s
and were lost to us in 2006

CONTENTS

ACKNOWLEDGEMENTS

To pull this work together my thanks begin with Michael Fry and all at the Tuesday Club for encouraging me to write rather than just talk – the lengths people will go to to shut me up for a few months! Graeme Brown, Peter Lyburn, Gingie Maynard, Alison Payne and Mirjam Seemke helped me reach the finishing line with a degree of punctuality that I could not have otherwise hoped for. Those have helped me develop novel ideas or talked me out of ridiculous notions that would not fly include Daniel Hannan, Geoff Mawdsley, Julia McIntyre, Andy McIver, Colin Robertson, Euan Wallace and Iain Whyte. Then there are the free market institutions, of which we need more in Scotland – Eamonn Butler at the Adam Smith Institute, Matthew Eliot at Taxpayers' Alliance, John Blundell and Philip Booth at the Institute of Economic Affairs, Andrew Haldenby at Reform, Tom Miers at the Policy Institute, Marion L. Tupy at the Cato Institute and Peter Young at Adam Smith International. I thank Eamonn and Christine Butler for letting me enjoy the sanctuary of their villa in Arran where I could actually read books and papers without fear of interruption and claim a poor cell-phone reception made contact impossible.

Finally I pay tribute to my family for their patience and give thanks to my publishers, Hugh Andrew and his team at Birlinn, for their patience and diligence, and the no doubt great launch party that is surely being organised as I type this last paragraph. Even if few Scots of influence are unwilling to believe or accept my arguments, I do anticipate there being much fun to be had debating them.

Introduction

CHALLENGING THE CONSENSUS

*'The point to remember is that what the
government gives it must first take away.'*
– JOHN S. COLEMAN

Reading the Scottish daily newspapers or surfing the news sites on the Internet can be a very depressing experience. A day never seems to pass without another politician or single-issue activist calling for more public funding that will require higher taxes here or a new tax there. Whether it is how to replace the unfair Council Tax or to alter our behaviour through the introduction of so-called green taxes, there is a modest industry of tax inventors and engineers seeking to extend the scope of the state and to require us to give it an ever-greater proportion of our wealth, no matter how poor people may be.

Devolution will always turn out to be more expensive to deliver than a single parliament at Westminster, and many of the policy outcomes, be they good or bad, would have been possible by changing political control at the Scottish Office. There is, however, no going back to the past system. I cannot express it better than Alan Massie when he wrote: 'Devolution is a reality that is here to stay. To dream or pretend otherwise is sheer Jacobitism: emotionally satisfying, practically pointless.'[1]

Despite the public's disenchantment with devolution I do still believe that it can be made to work far better than it is and so avoid independence becoming inevitable. While I agree with arch-unionist cheerleader Alan Cochrane that the Union represents 'the most successful alliance between two former enemies that the world has ever seen',[2] where I disagree with him and others of his ilk is about how it is to be preserved and given new life.

To do this requires Scotland to become part of the normal political debate that has dominated the parliaments of all Western economies in the last century – the struggle between a liberal open society and collectivist central planning. The degree to which the collectivist consensus has advanced in Scotland can be measured by the growth of the state and its public sector. The manner in which collectivism pervades all levels of society so that it is now the establishment is no better illustrated than by the incredulous position of CBI Scotland arguing that business rates should not be reduced below the English level – at a time when the Minister for Enterprise, Nicol Stephen, has been on record as advocating a competitive tax rate below England's. Only in Scotland would a business organisation argue that increased public spending is a good thing and that tax cuts for business are a bad thing.

This book is not, however, a balance sheet exercise for the lowering of Scottish taxation. It is about the pressures Scotland is likely to face, economically and politically, and what might be done to respond to them. It is about the moral case for lower taxes and the various options that could be tried. Public spending in Scotland will, I believe, face a variety of pressures in the next few years, including new spending restraints from London, threats to reform the Barnett Formula by way of a needs-based review reducing the Scottish block grant, and the dawning realisation of the need to find savings to finance modest tax cuts that can help invigorate the economy. It is about how we pay the public sector piper so he plays the public's tune – not one of his own making.

Nineteenth-century industrialisation created a brash new wealthy class that could buy power and it also created in its workers a demand for democratic rights. These two forces conspired to undermine the old moneyed families; the trick was to ensure that a new aristocracy did not simply replace the old one – that, through education and opportunity for all, the people who would in future wield power could come from any background. We were all meant to have a chance.

Since the 1800s successive legislation, taxation and social policy have ensured that our society is relatively open and meritocratic. There will always be people who wish to build new barriers to protect the gains that they have made, but so long as we observe the rule of law and respect people's property rights we can maintain our open and just society, which allows prosperity to be spread and enjoyed. Socialists and collectivists accuse supporters of a liberal capitalist order of seeking the rule of the jungle, but this is either ignorance or malevolence, for the vital component in an open society is the rule of law. Without such law, contracts will not be honoured and the weak will not be protected from powerful individuals, corporations or the state. Coupled with the rule of law must be the protection of property rights of the individual or of groups of people. The surest way that the smallest man or woman can stand up to anyone, be it the ruling class or the state, is by keeping what they earn. The spread of wealth, including the ability to hold assets such as your house, is crucial if we are to ensure that power and privilege is not concentrated in the hands of the few.

Half a century ago Friedrich Hayek argued that the biggest challenge for those who believe in 'the extended order' of free markets is winning the moral-cultural battle for a certain vision of society and he was, I believe, right, because it is a battle that is never ending. Hayek was, in a sense, advocating a permanent revolution, a Trotskyist approach to espousing liberal capitalism that would require the moral battle to be regularly fought, for there will always be new opponents and new adherents to be won.

Scotland is a good example of a country where people once understood how a liberal economy worked and had the entrepreneurial spirit and inventiveness to prove it, but has now become weakened and debilitated by the slow but certain addiction that comes with unchallenged welfare dependency, whether it has been economic support of failing industries, the well-intentioned planning of new ones or the intervention of government at every level of individual life – now from womb to grave.[3] In Scotland, advocates of an open liberal society, which will, by definition, allow capitalism to flourish under the rule of laws set by a democratic legislature, have either failed to articulate their case effectively enough or have failed to make it altogether. The sad irony that Scotland's own Enlightenment contributed so much to the understanding and shaping of an open liberal society is not lost on this author and has been the main reason for me wishing to do battle in Edinburgh rather than England. Such is the power of liberal ideas – still advancing in the developing world as socialism and its collectivist mutations retreat[4] – that it is never too late to propose them.

With every fresh generation there is a duty on those who supported Hayek when he wrote his great tracts, and then Ralph Harris and Arthur Seldon when they argued through the Institute of Economic Affairs, and now, when Matthew Elliot and James Frayne campaign through the Taxpayers' Alliance, to win over fresh converts. There are always new collectivists coming forward with fresh schemes that require the taxation of people to make them work – all for the good of society, of course. These schemes must be tested and challenged thoroughly before they are granted the benefit of having legal force behind them.

This battle cannot be materialistic but must be based upon the moral right of the individual to retain his or her fairly earned property and to use it as he or she wishes, within the context of our constantly evolving laws. Unfortunately, what we are witnessing now is, I believe, the complete abdication of that battle by politicians of the centre-right in Britain. David Cameron and George Osborne have, it would appear, walked off the battlefield and are willing to concede defeat to current levels of taxing and spending, or, more accurately, taxing and waste.

It is true that Margaret Thatcher did not in her 1979 general election manifesto make specific and detailed promises on tax cuts – and I have no beef with the Cameron and Osborne resistance to making specific and detailed pledges now or even in a future election campaign. She did, however, make it plain that tax cuts would come when they could be afforded and, to establish that she could be trusted, she and her lieutenants made the moral case for lower taxes.

This approach is in complete contrast to recent Conservative election campaigns, when all that William Hague and Michael Howard have done in each election is moan about stealth taxes; only providing an alternative tax strategy at the last minute. This approach can never be convincing as it has no moral appeal and plays to the accusations of 'same old Tories', only interested in the wealthy and not the poor.

Tax cuts are about emphasising the moral position of the individual in society to be free to act and interact without his or her property being confiscated – or they are no better than the vote buying that higher public spending so often is. Taxation is legalised theft and it must therefore be limited, constrained and always face pressure to be reduced, if not removed. Despite some theories of how society could succeed by voluntary means, the current view of society, and one that I do not see changing in my lifetime, is that there will always be the need for some taxation. The extent to which we accept taxation as a convenience must, however, be constantly confronted and the tendrils of this jungle hacked back. As people are released from taxation and enter into more contracts for themselves in the provision of education, healthcare, social services, and so on, so then taxation can be reduced further.[5]

The private interactions in providing and purchasing these currently nationalised services create new opportunities and innovations for learning, for healing and for caring. The provision of housing – which in the last hundred years has moved from a position where most people rented from a private landlord, to a position where they rented from a public landlord, to a position where they now own the property they live in – is a tangible and well understood example of how the market can liberate people and allow their taxes – which used to be used on subsidies to council housing and mortgage interest relief – to be reduced.

The same liberation that came to our eye care could happen to our dental care if only there was a political party willing to argue the moral and practical case, using the example that is the now wholly private provision of spectacles and contact lenses. Similar approaches in general medical provision would, I have no doubt, attract significant investment from the preferences of millions of people, enabling Britain's healthcare to develop solutions to our ailments more quickly. So taxation is not just about people being left to keep their money; it is about opening up the state monopolies of social provision so that people can choose to spend their money on their children's education or their parent's health-care – rather than on a second home in Spain, monoblock paving or the latest DIY fad to sweep the country. The state monopolies, whether they be centrally run or locally managed, limit the capacity of provision rather than support it. By encouraging more entrants to the markets so that there are more school places, hip replacements or care beds that can be purchased, the prices can fall and we can establish a virtuous cycle. As more provision transfers into the private sector, taxes can fall and private investment through purchasing can grow. These purchases are individual transactions where people have decided the location, the standard of service, the timing, the schoolbooks, the entertainment or whatever the many, many factors might be – rather than being subject to a well-meaning but entirely detached planner who has to aggregate and generalise in provision based on guestimates. The private choice is morally superior because it allows the person to make it rather than to be force-fed it and it does not require the confiscation of property in the form of taxes to deliver it.

In Britain the Forsyth Commission's report[6] on taxation has struck the right chord in recognising that tax cuts are about more than just benefiting those that pay taxes – but also helping the lowest paid and those who don't yet earn – by raising the incomes of the poor and bringing people back into employment through the creation of new jobs in a faster growing economy. Importantly, Forsyth's commission talked of tax *reform* rather than tax cutting – a crucial distinction if the sceptical and the doubters are to be won over. The type of tax cuts that the Forsyth Commission presented, and that I discuss here for Scotland, are just that – reforms that are designed not to benefit the wealthy but to change the emphasis of taxation so that the least well-off are taken out of tax altogether or find their taxes are less punitive and less regressive. If it so happens that wealthy people make significant savings in the course of things then why should I or anyone worry if, as always happens, they end up contributing more than they had before?

All politicians need to recognise is that tax cutting can liberate the poorest and weakest in society from dependency on the state so that they have the dignity of self-reliance and self-respect that so many of them seek. It is not about lining the pockets of the rich but about taking the hands of the state out of the pockets of the poor. The need for such action in Scotland, where the state is a greater intruder in our lives and in our businesses, is more pressing. For that reason and drawing on my past eight years' experience in Scottish politics, this book concentrates on what fiscal problems there are in Scotland and how, in addressing them, we can ensure responsibility and accountability in our institutions, revive public interest in the political process and invigorate our Scottish economy to the benefit of those who need it most.

NOTES

1. A. Massie: 'Change is the best option for the Status Quo', in *Scotland's Ten Tomorrows, The Devolution Crisis and how to solve it* (ed. B. Jamieson), Continuum, London, 2006.
2. Alan Cochrane, *Daily Telegraph*, 25 October 2006.
3. With the introduction of benefits to be paid to children not yet born and the maintenance of taxes on the dead, Chancellor Gordon Brown has literally extended the state's influence from cradle-to-grave to womb-to-grave.
4. Marc A. Miles, Kim R. Holmes and Mary Anastasia O'Grady: *2006 Index of Economic Freedom*, The Heritage Foundation, Washington DC and *The Wall Street Journal*, New York, 2006.
5. Man 'is more likely to give if he earns more than if he earns less. He earns more – and pays lower taxes – in a market than in a state economy. There is more selfless, voluntary giving in capitalism than in socialism', says Arthur Seldon in *The Virtues of Capitalism*. Taken to its logical conclusion, with lower and lower taxes man will give more and more until taxation might not be needed. The problem for governments is that the giving might not be in the areas it wishes. See Arthur Seldon: *The Virtues of Capitalism*, The Collected Works of Arthur Seldon, Liberty Fund, Indianapolis, 2004.
6. Michael Forsyth (Chairman): *Tax Matters, Reforming the Tax System*, Report of the Tax Reform Commission, London, 2006.

Chapter 1

THE WRONG TYPE OF GROWTH?

'for a nation to try to tax itself into prosperity is like a man standing in a bucket and trying to lift himself up by the handle'
– WINSTON CHURCHILL

If there is a section of the Scottish economy that it is growing it is the public sector. Nobody can deny that the growth in government spending in Scotland has been enormous. For adherents of greater public spending as a solution to our ills this will be welcomed but the independent evidence provided by the Auditor General, Robert Black, in his regular parliamentary reports shows that the resulting benefits that are talked about when the spending is announced to accompanying fanfares are often difficult to identify, if visible at all. For instance GPs, consultants and teachers have all had significant pay increases but the promised benefits to the consumers of improved services and expected productivity gains are elusive. Yes, the recipients report greater contentment, and so they should, but costs have been substantial.

The GP contract was estimated to incur annual costs of £575 million but the bill has turned out to be £623.7 million, with the new arrangements for out-of-hours cover the subject of regular controversy and significant public disquiet.[1]

According to Audit Scotland figures, the annual pay bill for consultants, prior to the new contract being introduced, was £257 million but this is projected to have risen by 44% to £370 million by 2005/06. The additional cost of the consultants' contract is expected to be £273 million over three years, a figure widely at variance with what the Scottish Executive expected.[2] In 2003 the Health Department originally underestimated the cost of the contract for the first three years by £171 million. In March 2004 the department's second estimate was still £32 million short. The NHS, under the management of Malcolm Chisholm throughout this period, was literally flying blind about the costs and without systems in place to quantify what benefits would come from the agreement. In November 2004, shortly after Andy Kerr replaced Chisholm, the department produced fresh figures but still underestimated the bill by £11 million, even though the contract was, by then, up and running, having been introduced that year but backdated to March 2003 the previous year. This one-off back payment alone cost £76 million. The Auditor General said of the contract: 'Prior to the introduction of the new contract, the Scottish Executive Health Department (SEHD) set out a number of anticipated benefits for the NHS in Scotland. However, it has not provided timely guidance to ensure these benefits were planned for from the outset . . . 'It has the potential to improve patient care, but there is not yet clear evidence of benefits.'

The teachers' agreement that was the result of the McCrone recommendations displayed very similar failings to that of the consultant and GP contracts. Audit Scotland reported in 2006 that local authorities had spent an estimated £2.15 billion in implementing the agreement, which delivered a 23% increase to all teachers costing £1.64 billion.[3] The Auditor General was not sparing in the lack of value for money benefits accruing from the deal: 'It is difficult to assess the extent to which value for money has been achieved from the additional spending because clear outcome measures were not included in the Agreement and have not yet been put in place by the Scottish Executive and other parties to the Agreement.'

If anyone had any doubts as to the scale of the Scottish

Executive's failings in measuring expected benefits he listed the specific outcome measures that were absent but could have been included: 'impact on educational attainment; improvements in classroom practice; the quality of educational leadership; workload and skill-mix; workforce morale; and recruitment and retention within the profession.'

During the Scottish Parliament Audit Committee's[4] own inquiry into the teachers' agreement, the Scottish Executive admitted that the information the Executive used to estimate what funds would be required was 'not as complete as we would have desired it to be' and that it had underestimated costs by £51.5 million.[5] Fortunately, the Education Department spent £34.8 million less than its final estimates – but as this was due to unexpected variances in the agreement's introduction, such as the employment of fewer support staff and the slow take-up of the Chartered Teacher Scheme, it appears to have been a case of good fortune and not better management than the Health Department.

It is not as if there have not been warnings from a number of quarters. Writing in the *Scottish Left Review*[6] on why devolution could damage the prospects for the SNP achieving Scottish Independence, economists Jim and Margaret Cuthbert said:

> There has been the failure of the new parliament to establish proper financial responsibility and control. The most visible example of this has been Holyrood: but there have been other mistakes, and some are arguably even more damaging: for example, the way in which new financial controls for Scottish Water were implemented, leading to serious overcharging: the inadequate costing of free personal care for the elderly: the laxity in the way in which the McCrone agreement on teachers' pay and conditions was introduced and, perhaps most significant of all, the failure to recognise the gravity of the financial situation facing the health service.

It should be appreciated that the Cuthberts wrote this analysis before having the benefit of the Auditor General's reports on free personal care, the teachers' agreement, the consultant's contract and the financial overview of the NHS that subsequently vindicated their stance generally.

Given the scale and pace of the growth in Scottish public spending such laxity should maybe not be surprising to seasoned observers. When the Scottish Parliament came into being Scottish Executive spending, which is funded by the Scottish block grant and business rates, stood at £15.6 billion. Six years later, after Gordon Brown's various spending reviews and additional spending, financed by some visibly higher and many less visible indirect stealth taxes, Scottish Executive spending stood at £25.8 billion and is planned to reach £30 billion by 2007 (see Tables at end of chapter). Of course the electorate has voted for more teachers, nurses, doctors and police, and it is only right, therefore, that they are delivered. The figures, however, when broken down tell another story: we find that more administrative staff have been hired in the NHS than doctors, nurses and clinicians put together.

Another example of the growth in government spending is the expansion of public servants. The Scottish Executive alone has seen its complement increase from 3,677 in 1999 to 4,410 by 2005. The costs have ballooned from £152 million in 1999 to £234 million by 2005. Not to be outdone, the redundant Scottish Office has seen its complement rise from 73 in 1999 to 130 in 2003–04 – almost double.

The growth in directly employed government employees is not restricted to the Scottish Executive or the Scottish Office. The figures for civil servants employed in Scotland by UK departments and agencies, but excluding the Scottish Parliament, the Scottish Business Ombudsman and the Office of the Scottish Charity Regulator, has also grown. In the first quarter of 1999 the complement stood at 48,300 but by the last quarter of 2005 it had reached 51,800 – an increase of 3,500 (more than the Ravenscraig steelworks workforce in the 1980s). The total numbers for public sector employment have risen from 524,600 in the first quarter of 1999 to 580,300 in the last quarter of 2005. That is an increase of 55,264, representing a 10.6% growth.

Scottish Executive increase in staff

	1999	2000	2001	2002	2003	2004	2005
Staff numbers	3,677	3,926	3,965	4,290	4,272	4,393	4,410
Admin (£m)	152	175	200	208	219	225	234

Year ending 31st March

In 2004/05 England's total identifiable current expenditure on services was £5,893 per head compared with £7,020 in Scotland. By 2005 all but one government department in Scotland was spending more per head than its equivalent department in England, that sole department being Public Order and Safety, which is highly distorted by London's security commitments. As I have already mentioned, the benefits of greater spending are not always obvious, if they exist at all. On enterprise and economic development Scotland spends £82 per head while England spends £56 per head and yet there were 28 business start-ups per 10,000 people in Scotland, compared with 38 in England in 2005.[7] Indeed in many areas of public services where Scotland's spending is higher the outputs are poorer. Why? Has state dependency sapped Scotland's legendary work ethic?

No one with Scotland's interests at heart can seriously argue that such a high proportion of public spending is desirable, sustainable or is anything but a heavy drag on the country's economic performance, especially compared to England. A cross-country empirical study by R.J. Barro[8] showed how high public spending can lead to reduced economic growth, with a 1% increase in government spending being associated with a 0.14% retardation in the growth of real GDP. This might seem an insignificant figure, but when applied by David B. Smith,[9] economist at Wiliams De Broe, to the 10% growth in UK public spending since 1960 it results in lower economic growth of 1.3% – a significant amount. Consider then that Scotland's public spending is about 25% larger than England's and it is difficult to deny that our economic growth is likely to be disadvantaged. Scotland's economic growth relative to the rest of the UK is consistently behind England's average. In the year to the first quarter of 2005 it was 2.0% compared with 2.7% – and Cambridge Econometrics is predicting growth at 2.0% for 2006 and 2.25% for 2007 – both behind the UK average and that of many English regions.[10]

The degree to which the public sector depresses Scottish economic performance can best be gauged by Scotland's rank against England in the 2006 IMD World Competitiveness League.[11] Given that Scotland operates with the same trade regime, same employment law, same corporation tax, income tax and many other taxes one might expect the two countries to be reasonably close. Such an expectation would, however, be wrong; Scotland is placed at 30, behind the UK at 21. Given that Scotland's figures are included within the UK average, it must be that England will be even further ahead, nearer the top 10.

The deadweight that Scotland's private sector has to carry and that puts it at a competitive disadvantage is not just theoretical. As the Scottish Parliament's Enterprise and Culture Committee has reported, Scotland lags behind its UK and Organisation for Economic Co-operation and Development (OECD) competitors when its economic performance is measured against a number of key factors. David Bell, professor of economics at the University of Stirling, has calculated that the private sector in Scotland has grown by only 12.8% since 1998, while the public sector has expanded by 19.3%, which means that Scotland's private sector is stuck in the slow lane. Peter MacMahon, writing in *The Scotsman*,[12] said Professor Bell's figures reveal that 'The public sector GVA has grown by 20.7 per cent in the UK and 19.3 per cent in Scotland. But the private sector has risen by 20.1 per cent in the UK, against just 12.8 per cent in Scotland.'

There is not a great deal of difference between the figures for the public sector, but there is a significant difference between those for the private sector. Professor Bell said: 'The gap between rates of growth in the UK and in Scotland is almost entirely explained by the gap in performance of the private sector.' He warned that, given the slowdown in the amount of money that Scotland will receive from the Treasury, 'future growth will be dependent on increasing the economic health of Scotland's private sector'. Scotland has had the wrong type of growth and, if it is to avoid significant social upset and discord when the Treasury's expected financial belt-tightening comes, it needs private sector growth badly, and fast.

How then do we give businesses the incentive to become more active, for more companies to be formed, for Scotland's entre-preneurial spirit to be reawakened? Fortunately we can reverse this process by changing the culture of enterprise in Scotland so that more people see their economic prospects as being better here than elsewhere. We can change the mentality that it is better to find a relatively safe salaried job in the dominant public sector than to set up a business or work in the riskier private sector. We can make Scotland attractive to economic migrants, but this cannot be done by spending more money on public services – migrants don't come for public services; they come for better economic prospects. Nor should the Government and its agencies be bringing forward more initiatives that nominate businesses or sectors to stimulate growth. That approach prolongs the dependency on state intervention and 'government knows best' ethos that is anathema to the development of an enterprise culture and has taken us to our current perilous position. It can only be done by making Scotland a more competitive 'can do' economy by reducing the costs to business. Period.

It has to be stated that, as there has already been a differential in the ratios between the growth of the public and private sectors in Scotland and the rest of the UK, to reverse the ratios will require changes in what we do in Scottish policy, rather than Treasury policy. While the Treasury's policy for England is responsible for the Barnett Formula delivering ever-growing budgets to the Scottish Executive, it is how the Executive has deployed the largesse that is the vital factor in seeing the disproportionate growth in Scotland's public sector. It therefore requires a focus on what can be done in Scotland – and if there is a lack of options or powers to respond then unionists such as myself have to face up to the question: how we can address the problems in a Scottish context without risking full independence?

I would welcome proper restraints on spending and the reform, if not the abolition, of the Barnett Formula so that the private sector would have an incentive and greater room to grow. More importantly, I think that the economy requires more than just modest tax cuts at the margins. The task is not just to nudge the economy but to change the country's culture, lifting it from its relative torpor so it becomes the entrepreneurial centre of the UK, second only to London – an ambitious but realistic goal. This will require significant and sustained tax reform. For that to happen also requires that savings, through efficiencies and changes in spending plans, will have to be found – a political journey that is always difficult, but even more so in a country now run by coalition governments.

I make no attempt here to itemise what programmes should be trimmed or abandoned and what new initiatives that might require spending to bring savings should be introduced – and I make no apologies for this. To bring about tax cuts *will* require changes in spending plans but studies elsewhere and by no less than the Executive itself are regularly appearing and suggest a whole range of options. My point is simple: if the Executive can identify efficiency gains and underspends that it can return to departments to spend all over again then I have absolutely no doubt that the same measures would bring savings of current and capital account spending that could be returned to the taxpayer instead.

Furthermore, a range of political decisions could bring further savings and here, for the purpose of illustration, I turn to the work of Professor Sir Donald MacKay and Professor David Bell in their Policy Institute paper, *The Political Economy of Devolution*,[13] which lists a variety of measures that could reduce spending by the Scottish Executive by £3 billion – before the addition of the Executive's own efficiency gains. These proposals include maintaining spending on pupils and students at current per capita levels, but using the fall in school and college rolls to bring education spending down: 'Thus, just holding spending per pupil or student constant, and letting spending follow Scottish demographic trends would save around £429 million per year. Rationalisation of provision could add at least £25m to that total.'

Identifying best practices and driving management costs closer to the best 25% performing boards suggest savings of £500m in the NHS could be obtained. The privatisation of Scottish Water could, they suggest, raise £2 billion and relieve the Executive of £260 million annual costs. The former amount I am sceptical about, such is the debt structure of Scottish Water, but the annual running costs have been identified by others, including the Scottish Conservatives, who are suggesting using it to reduce Council Tax for pensioners. Other suggestions include:

> cutting back on the Executive's advertising budget that has more than tripled since devolution; reducing the number of ministers; cutting the number of special advisers to the Executive and tsars; making greater use of e-procurement than is envisaged under the efficient government review to save a further £400m; extending prison privatisation, which could save £100m a year; privatising the Forestry Commission and Forest Enterprise Scotland, which costs £80m; cutting back on the Executive's international relations budget, which is now worth £30m; making greater use of contracting out of services; cutting back on the Caledonian Macbrayne subsidy or perhaps privatising it. Together these should be capable of generating savings of over £600m.

Taking all of these suggestions together brings MacKay and Bell close to the £3 billion previously mentioned, although I would discount the suggested £212 million savings on servicing the debt on council housing because the housing revenue account is separate from local government finances and any savings go to the tenants, not the councils. Mackay and Bell are not naïve about the difficulty of delivering such savings, stating: 'implementing these savings would be politically unpopular . . . there would certainly be a requirement to phase the changes in over, say, a period of five years.'

Given that MacKay and Bell have not included the Executive's own efficiency gains or allowed for the introduction of fresh income streams, such as top-up fees for those universities that would like to charge them, the target of building towards a £3 billion reduction in spending that would allow both the phasing out of business rates and a 3p cut in income tax using the Tartan Tax is eminently realistic. As I explain in Chapter 4, a cut in income tax would initiate a review of the Barnett Formula so that Scotland's per capita spending is brought closer to English levels, although probably still being higher. So long as the Barnett Formula – or a reformed version of it – was in place this reduction could be achieved by slowing or freezing the growth in public spending so that it was not as fast as that of England. Over a period of five to ten years the difference in per capita spending in the two countries could then be significantly altered.

Of course if fiscal autonomy were in place this question would be handled differently as borrowing would be part of the arrangement, as would the accrual to a Scottish Treasury of additional revenues that tax reforms could generate.[14] Indeed the whole foregoing exercise in planning for savings and spending efficiencies has not taken account of the Laffer effect, whereby cutting the marginal rates in taxes can increase government revenues by encouraging greater productivity and consumption – and therefore the possibility of growing revenues allowing spending to be maintained at broadly the same levels. This is intentional on my part, for while I firmly believe this outcome is eminently achievable I believe that to carry the argument in Scotland you have to show that you are prepared for increased tax revenues not happening. What follows is consideration of how public spending might be better controlled in Scotland through a more fiscally responsible system that goes hand in hand in driving down taxes, whether you believe in the Laffer curve or not.

NOTES
1. Parliamentary Question S2W-29577, 21 November 2006, by Derek Brownlee.
2. Auditor General for Scotland: *Implementing the NHS consultant contract in Scotland*, Auditor General for Scotland, Edinburgh, 2006.
3. Auditor General for Scotland, *A mid-term report – A first stage review of the cost and implementation of the teachers' agreement*, Auditor General for Scotland, Edinburgh, 2006.
4. The author is convener of this committee.
5. Scottish Parliament Audit Committee, 7th Report Session 2, *A mid-term report – a first stage review of the cost and implementation of the teachers' agreement*, Edinburgh, 2006.
6. Jim and Margaret Cuthbert: 'Opposing but not imposing', *Scottish Left Review* 24, September/October 2004.
7. www.sbs.gov.uk/SBS_Gov_files/researchandstats/VATStatsPressReleaseOct 2006.pdf.
8. R.J. Barro, *Determinants of Economic Growth: A Cross Country Empirical Study*, MIT Press, Cambridge MA, 1997.

9. David B. Smith: *Leaving with Leviathan: Public Spending, Taxes and Economic Performance*, The Institute of Economic Affairs, 17 November 2006.
10. Office of National Statistics, and Cambridge Econometrics: *Regional Economic Prospects*, August 2006.
11. 2006 IMD World Competitiveness League, International Institute of Management Development, Lausanne.
12. Peter MacMahon, *The Scotsman*, 24 February 2006.
13. Mackay, Sir Donald and Bell, David: *The Political Economy of Devolution*, The Policy Institute, Edinburgh, September 2006.
14. The whole range of options is fully discussed by Ross Harper and Iain Stewart: *Paying Our Way: Should Scotland raise its own taxes?*, The Policy Institute, Edinburgh, December 2003.

Government expenditure

Year	Scottish Office Spending	Scottish Executive Spending	Total Gov Spending (Identifiable)
1996–1997	£14.3 billion	NA	£31.8 bn (£24.7bn)
1997–1998	£14.7 billion	NA	£32.1 bn (£24.4bn)
1998–1999	NA	£15.6 billion	£33.4 bn (£25.7bn)
1999–2000	NA	£16.5 billion	£34.1 bn (£27.0bn)
2000–2001	NA	£17.6 billion	£36.5 bn (£28.4bn)
2001–2002	NA	£19.6 billion	£39.4 bn (£31.6bn)
2002–2003	NA	£22.4 billion	£40.9 bn (£33.3bn)
2003–2004	NA	£24.8 billion	£45.3 bn (£37.2bn)
2004–2005	NA	£25.8 billion	£47.7 bn (£38.6bn)

Identifiable Expenditure is defined as expenditure that can be identified as having been incurred for the benefit of the population of a particular country/region such as Defence, Public Order and Safety, Enterprise and economic development, science and technology, employment policies, Agriculture/fisheries/forestry, Transport, Environment protection, Housing and community amenities, Health, Recreation / culture / religion, education / training, social protection.

Non-identifiable Expenditure Non-identifiable expenditure includes General public services, EU transactions, International services, Debt interest, Defence, Public order and safety, Enterprise and economic development, Science and technology, Employment policies, Agriculture/fisheries/forestry, Transport, Environment protection, Housing and community amenities, Health, Recreation/culture/religion, Education/training, and Social Protection.

[Source: Scottish Executive GERS]

Government revenue

Year	Total government revenues for Scotland	Revenue from business rates in Scotland	% of total revenue	United Kingdom revenues from oil
1996–1997	£24.7 billion	£1.2 billion	4.86%	£3.5 billion
1997–1998	£26.7 billion	£1.3 billion	4.87%	£3.3 billion
1998–1999	£28.2 billion	£1.4 billion	4.96%	£2.6 billion
1999–2000	£29.8 billion	£1.5 billion	5.03%	£2.5 billion
2000–2001	£30.9 billion	£1.6 billion	5.18%	£4.3 billion
2001–2002	£31.4 billion	£1.7 billion	5.41%	£5.2 billion
2002–2003	£31.6 billion	£1.7 billion	5.38%	£4.9 billion
2003–2004	£34.0 billion	£1.7 billion	5.00%	£4.3 billion
2004–2005	£36.4 billion	£1.8 billion	4.95%	£5.2 billion

[Source: Scottish Executive GERS]

Public sector and the work force

Year	Economically active UK (millions)	Economically active Scotland (millions)	% Public Sector in UK	% Public Secvtor in Scotland
1999–2000	28.987	2.474	19.2%	23.0%
2000–2001	29.087	2.516	19.2%	22.6%
2001–2002	29.297	2.510	19.4%	22.6%
2002–2003	29.588	2.542	19.7%	22.9%
2003–2004	29.712	2.543	20.0%	23.0%
2004–2005	30.004	2.600	20.3%	23.2%
2005–2006	30.310	2.603	20.4%	23.5%
2006–2007	30.615	2.596	20.2%	NA

[Source: ONS Labour Force Projections, January 2006]

Chapter 2

WHO PAYS THE PIPER?

'Taxation with representation ain't so hot either.'
— GERALD BARZAN

Effects of the Barnett Formula

The reason for Scotland's high public expenditure is easy to identify – it is the existing funding mechanism whereby a block grant is given from the Treasury to the Scottish Executive, adjusted annually by a calculation called the Barnett Formula, a name coined by Professor David Heald after the former Labour Chief Secretary to the Treasury, Joel Barnett, who introduced it. Previous calculations had been based upon the Goschen Formula, first devised in the 1880s to deal with the financing of Irish home rule. The formula does not reallocate existing expenditure but provides for the adjustments in English spending in departments that were devolved onto the former Scottish Office and now the Scottish Executive. Put simply, a calculation is made to increase or decrease Scottish spending by a percentage based upon the population ratio between Scotland and England. The formula has no legislative force but is a convention[1] and so it can be adjusted with relative ease, although significant changes would provoke a political outcry from whoever were the losers.

Although there are circumstances when the Barnett Formula can result in a reduction of the block grant, such as when public expenditure is cut in the UK, such occurrences are rare. The outcome is that there is no incentive to make savings (as they will attract a cut in the Scottish block grant by the Treasury in the following year's budget allocation – just as any other department's underspend would). All the incentives are towards spending the full allocation and this often involves the invention of new spending programmes, new initiatives and new institutions which, by their very creation, require the funding to continue, thus creating a public spending ratchet effect which only goes one way – up!

Any attempt to reduce spending in Scotland is fraught with difficulty: the beneficiaries all have their single-issue pressure groups which argue that in fact more spending is required, not less. Spending reductions are considered socially painful and politically risky and politicians are therefore likely to suggest them only at the margins.

The creation of the Scottish Parliament and the introduction by it of Scotland's own Auditor General, informed by Audit Scotland, and the Parliament's Audit Committee has of course brought a level of scrutiny to the spending of public finances that was not possible at Westminster. The Executive's budget is scrutinised by the Finance Committee, helped by a team of advisors, while every subject committee (such as Education or Health) reviews the budget proposals of the departments it covers and feeds into the Finance Committee's deliberations – although the degree to which they are capable of doing this is highly questionable. Despite these most welcome and appropriate lengths of scrutiny there remains, however, little opportunity for politicians of either the ruling or opposition parties to use these processes to develop alternative spending priorities that will reduce spending.

If, like me, one believes that the level of public spending in Scotland is too high, and if one believes that some incentives must be in place to arrest, if not reverse, the growth in public spending in

Scotland, then it must be accepted as vital that the block grant and the Barnett Formula be replaced – for it is now working against Scotland's economic and social interests. I'm not arguing for the current system to be abolished overnight. Some transfer of funds from Westminster to Edinburgh would undoubtedly continue in the short to medium term, but the formula will need to be adjusted or phased out,[2] especially if Scottish taxes are ever cut, so we should not feel uncomfortable about discussing what that new formula might be.

From the perspective of many people in England the Scottish block grant gives Scotland an unfair public spending advantage. Yes, Scotland has significant areas of deprivation and a large number of remote communities, but there is deprivation in England too and there has been much change in economic development and population movement since 1978 without the formula being reviewed. It is not unreasonable to believe that any 'needs-based' review would see Scotland lose a share of its funding to other areas in the United Kingdom – which is why it was always resisted by Scottish Office Ministers (Conservative or Labour). The move from Goschen to Barnett and subsequent Barnett adjustments[3] have already seen the fraction of UK spending passed on to the Scottish Office or Scottish Executive change as the populations have changed. This process is likely to continue as regular adjustments to population proportions are now standard practice.

English politicians have also been scared to offend the Scots by reducing spending in Scotland as a result of the quite legitimate effects of the Barnett Formula. One of the most absurd examples of this was in the general election of 2005 when Shadow Chancellor of the Exchequer, Oliver Letwin MP, shied away from admitting his spending plans would reduce the Scottish block grant, even though he had announced as policy a deceleration of spending in England and Wales. Despite that, the Conservatives would 'increase the Scottish block grant at exactly the same rate as Labour'. At the time I was Conservative Finance spokesman and I had little alternative but to welcome the announcement, although it was not the course of action that I would have recommended.[4]

As well as promoting the growth of public spending in Scotland the Barnett formula actually discourages the use of the tax variation of up to 3p allowable under the Scotland Act, commonly known as the Tartan Tax, in any way other than to *raise* the standard rate of tax. This is because the Treasury policy is that if tax is raised by, say, 3p in the pound, it will deliver about £870 million to the Treasury (roughly £290 million per 1p). Conversely, if the tax rate is cut by 3p the Treasury believes that it will lose £870 million and accordingly would reduce the block grant by this amount to compensate. The premise that cutting tax should mean less revenue need not, however, be the case. A cut in income tax could be expected to improve Scottish productivity; it could bring retired people back into the economy and attract wealth-creating migrants to work in Scotland. All of these factors would increase tax revenues. Unfortunately, under the current arrangements any increased revenues would go to the Treasury (see Chapter 4).

The Barnett Formula, which in its conception was meant to bring about convergence between Scottish and English public spending, remains a subject of debate between academics, who dispute whether or not it is achieving this aim.[5] The work by Professor David Bell[6] explains the concept of the Barnett 'squeeze' and how variations in population can reverse (or indeed accelerate) the outcome. With a declining population[7] the effect is to reverse the squeeze and leave spending with much the same per capita differential that it had. The recent influx of migrant workers from the EU may have an impact on the Barnett Formula if the proportions between Scotland and England change significantly.

However, as it is now becoming clear that spending growth is unlikely to be maintained at recent levels, this, together with the unpredictability of the population movements, leads me to suggest that for the moment the Barnett squeeze should generally be ignored as a distraction from the larger problem of the lack of restraint on public spending *in Scotland*.

Scotland's block grant is the elephant in the room at the debating chambers of Westminster and Holyrood that no one will acknowledge; it is the birthday suit that all Emperors eat, sleep and drink in without a second thought. No courtiers or pretenders to the throne dare say anything, for they too are wearing a suit cut of the same cloth. Be they Treasury ministers, First ministers or junior ministers it's time for a change of tailor. The Barnett Formula must go in its current form, as it is no longer in Scotland's interests.

The origins of fiscal autonomy

In the spring of 1988 the Scottish Conservative and Unionist Party held its annual conference at Perth, the first such event since a thoroughly demoralising defeat at the general election of June 1987. While Margaret Thatcher had won her record-breaking third term in office[8] with a UK majority of 102 her Scottish colleagues had seen their number diminish from 22 to 10 and the majorities of the remaining seats slashed. The Scottish Conservatives were in serious trouble and agreement about how best to respond had to be found.

There was a small group of prominent members that believed the best hope of a Conservative revival was for the party to bring forward proposals for home rule. At a Tory Reform Group conference fringe meeting a paper was launched by Michael Fry (*Scotsman* journalist and Conservative candidate in East Lothian, who edited the work), Quintin Jardine (former Tory press officer about to become a popular crime novelist), Ross Leckie (former candidate) and councillors Brian Meek and Struan Stevenson. The paper outlined how a Scottish Parliament might take shape and why it should have tax-raising powers.[9]

The Parliament would be responsible for the collection of all taxes in Scotland and a precept would be paid to Westminster for common services such as social welfare benefits, defence and foreign affairs. This was the moment the idea of full fiscal freedom was born in modern Scottish politics. It was not a nationalist invention dreamt up as a stepping-stone to independence; it was conceived as a new structure to rededicate Scotland's place in the Union and halt what was feared would otherwise be an inevitable separation of a socialist Scotland from a free market Britain. Although popular with the media, the paper of 1987 received short shrift from the conference representatives and in a full conference debate only nine out of 300 people supported even the concept of some type of home rule.

The work of Fry *et al.* did not, however, go unrewarded. In 1997 in Glasgow, again at the first Scottish Conservative conference held since the Tory wipe-out of that year, the Tuesday Club[10] published its first pamphlet, entitled *Full Fiscal Freedom,* co-authored by a young Murdo Fraser.[11] In a new mood of free expression, helped by the fact that there were no MPs before whom the usually deferential Tory party members could prostrate themselves, the pamphlet found many admirers. The cause of fiscal autonomy within the Union was about to gain supporters.

This was, of course, only the beginning of the debate that would illustrate the difficulty Conservatives north and south of the border would have in coming to terms with Donald Dewar's devolution cocktail. The debate has since gathered momentum, despite considerable attempts by Scottish Tory leaders, David McLetchie and his successor Annabel Goldie, to either keep it off their agenda or downplay its importance for fear of dividing the party.

There have been many Tory advocates for fiscal autonomy both within the Conservative group of MSPs at Holyrood and among commentators in the Scottish and British press. Although many Conservative MSPs will not openly reveal their true thoughts for fear of embarrassing their various leaders, I have no doubt that a majority of them actually support the idea. Columnists such as Alan Massie, Michael Gove and Dan Hannan have all brought the idea to a wider British public and converts appear regularly, for example Katie Grant, writing in *The Scotsman*. Lined up against these advocates are Gerald Warner and Alan Cochrane, whose attacks stop short of calling for the abolition of the Scottish Parliament – but only just.

Warner has a habit of calling Conservatives who serve in the Scottish Parliament 'Vichy Tories' or the 'craven clique'.[12] In one of his occasional Edwardian eviscerations of fiscal autonomy, and in particular the Tories that advocate it, Warner says: 'A Scottish parliament with unrestricted tax-raising powers would turn this country into a Trotskyite slum within five years', and so asks the question: 'do you want Rosie Kane setting your taxes?'[13] Warner turns a blind eye to the fact that as an MSP Rosie already has the power to vote for higher taxes – through bringing forward her own member's bill, pressing for a rise in the standard rate of income tax (the Tartan Tax) or hiking up business rates. The reality is that she is never likely to have the support to do it and there is no evidence that suggests the Trots, or even Labour or the SNP, now have the appetite for the fiscal rape of the Scottish people. Still, raising the spectre of Rosie Kane in charge of taxation no doubt politically titillated a few Bishopton Belles, which is what *Scotland on Sunday* has always paid Warner to do.

Taxpayers are, of course, not limited to just those that pay income taxes. Fiscal autonomy is likely to mean the ability of the Scottish Parliament to vary other taxes such as VAT, possibly excise duties, stamp duties and inheritance tax. The effect of setting levels of a broad range of taxes would undoubtedly lead to some differences with the rest of the United Kingdom but the effect of tax competition with a neighbour ten times as big would, I suggest, have a very sobering effect on those who might think they could behave like drunks in charge of a brewery. Yes, there are very many rabidly red nationalists wanting full independence, but if you look at the people advocating fiscal autonomy they are pretty much to a man and woman blue-blooded tax cutters. Warner also suggests that fiscal autonomy would fail to bring accountability in the same way that the Council Tax has failed to make Scotland's local authorities accountable. The lack of local accountability – a problem that stalks the whole of the United Kingdom – is precisely because of the *lack* of fiscal autonomy of local councils, not because of it. Council Tax covers only 16.7% of Scottish council spending, hardly enough of a council's budget to make the electorate appreciate what they are voting for – or councillors care what they think. Introduce a system that ensures the local electorate has to meet the majority of a council's running costs and just watch the electorate marching off to the polls to throw out those laying waste to their hard-earned income.

Warner's argument that sovereignty provides taxation and that therefore a tax-raising fiscally autonomous Scottish Parliament must be a sovereign parliament of an independent state is a *non sequitur*.[14] A brief look around Europe and North America will reveal states in America, provinces in Canada, laender in Germany and the Bund in Switzerland that, within the sovereignty of their states, have been delegated powers to tax corporate transactions and profits, personal incomes and the consumption that stems from it. Even smaller counties, districts and communities have in turn been delegated powers from those intermediate jurisdictions to raise charges or taxes too. Yes, the power of the rule of law that stems from a sovereign parliament is necessary to confiscate liquid or solid assets and call it a tax, but the same sovereign parliament can also allow that power to be exercised by other bodies, and it is delusional to suggest such arrangements require states to be ripped asunder when there are many countries that have existed in this manner for not just years, but centuries.

Former Scottish Secretaries Malcolm Rifkind, Ian Lang and Michael Forsyth all speak from the same hymn sheet in defending the Barnett Formula, supported by former minister Raymond Robertson. Other ex-ministers such as Alan Stewart and Peter Fraser recognise the arrival of the Parliament requires change to the current financial arrangements. Writing in *The Sunday Times*, Fraser, who was director of the No No campaign in 1997, described the current arrangements as 'inherently unstable' and argued that 'the only logical step' was to give the Scottish Parliament more powers: 'it's clear there's a mood in England that wonders why they're paying for Scotland. I think that's why there's a powerful argument that what we spend we should raise in Scotland, based on taxation.' [15]

It was never realistic to expect that the Tory party would rush headlong from a policy of complete and utter opposition to any form of parliamentary devolution towards one that went further than the Labour and Liberal Democrat parties had originally offered. Nevertheless, the Tories delay in opening to its membership the opportunity to weigh up a serious of options which might range from calling for the Scottish Parliament's abolition (still advocated by a small if shrinking group of activists) to a fully blown fiscally autonomous parliament, as originally envisaged by Fry *et al.* and then Murdo Fraser – possibly informed by an official policy commission like those recently established by David Cameron – has allowed other politicians such as Andrew Wilson and Jim Mather in the SNP and Jeremy Purvis in the Liberal Democrats to present the policy as their own. Subsequently, the Steel Commission Report[16] recommended to Liberal Democrats a form of fiscal autonomy, branded as fiscal federalism, which was adopted in principle as party policy.

Accepting devolution is here to stay is not enough for the Tories, as Allan Massie has argued in a number of his columns and essays.

Nor is coming out with empty slogans such as 'making devolution work' – especially when it translates to keeping Labour in power. Surely if Conservatives think devolution is broke and requires fixing then 'voting blue to get red' does not begin to address the real issues? Allan Massie sums up the situation well when describing the startled Tory party caught in the headlights of an approaching constitutional collision, not knowing whether to go left, right or to jump on board: 'it has accepted the reality, it has not yet embraced it. It has not yet addressed itself to the question: how do we make this unwanted Parliament function effectively?'[17]

If the Tory party does not address the Parliament's failings in a strategic manner then it will end up as roadkill – and it will have been its own fault. It is an open debate that the party cannot ignore for much longer. By the time that David Cameron fights the British parliamentary elections, some time before the summer of 2010, the Conservatives must finally have decided how to address the desire for reform of Holyrood, together with growing discontent amongst the English electorate. Even an opinion poll in the *Sunday Telegraph* that showed majority support on both sides of the border in favour of Scottish independence – whatever the respondents might have thought that term meant – has not woken up the somnambulant Conservatives. To ignore the issue will be to pass by the chance to redefine the party as truly Scottish and leave the threat from nationalists unanswered. Advocating fiscal autonomy will not in itself bring thousands of votes to the Conservatives; it will, however, make all its other policies on finance and public services relevant.

As far as I am concerned, devolution is here to stay. We cannot run around setting up parliaments one moment and abolishing them the next. The Scottish people voted for the principle of devolution in 1997, and we should respect their decision on the principle. Arguments that the numbers were not great enough are nothing other than the mean spirit of bad losers. The structure of the Holyrood institution was, of course, delivered from the deliberations of the Constitutional Convention and without the official participation of either the Scottish National Party or Scottish Conservative Party – usually representing together nearly 50% of the electorate. It is fair to say that the devolution model we have is Labour's model, delivered at the cost of including proportional representation to gain the support of the Liberal Democrats. While significant change to Labour's Scotland Act could arguably require the endorsement of a further referendum, devolution should not be seen as beyond fair and reasonable reform following informed debate.

It was suggested by many of its advocates in August and September 1997 that what was being proposed in Donald Dewar's devolution white paper would offer a radical departure from the supposedly outmoded politics of Westminster. On the contrary, what passes for debate and scrutiny at Holyrood is not so much a new politics as greater scope for bad, even frivolous, legislation compared to what the more disciplined procedures and fiscal accountability of Westminster produce. What our devolutionary settlement tells the Scottish people to do is to get themselves organised into pressure groups, to shout as loudly as possible for the interests of their pressure groups, regardless of any wider effect on Scottish society, and to build up such a political momentum for change that it becomes easier for the Scottish Executive to give in than to resist. A typical example is the Children's Commissioner, lobbied for by children's welfare charities.

This is also why, not very far down the line, the Scottish Executive ends up extending its financial commitments beyond its original priorities. The lack of financial pressures to rein back spending is also reflected in the bargaining between parties that enter into the Executive coalition. The Liberal Democrats will, for instance, have in their manifesto commitments policies such as free eye tests and free dental checks for all, with the real cost being paid to the health professionals out of the NHS budget. The main beneficiaries of this welfarism are not the poorest in society – who are already receiving such services free because they are under sixteen, in full time education, of pensionable age or in receipt of housing benefit – no, the main beneficiaries are the middle class Liberal Democrat voters who were already paying for the services. Labour will not have included these electoral bribes in its manifesto (every party has its own inducements) but will accept them as a clause of the partnership agreement – after all, the block grant will pay for it. The political imperative is to strike a deal and straighten out the funding later, conscious of the fact that any downward pressure on spending is barely visible and is less than the pressure to achieve power. Labour introduced free golf lessons for all schoolchildren; next on the Liberal Democrats' agenda for 2007 will be free swimming lessons.

Of course, for unionist politicians of any political hue fiscal freedom has always presented a political paradox in that it appears to take Scotland far closer to independence than unionists have wanted to in the past or might be expected to contemplate. This calls for surefooted and audacious leadership – a combination in short supply at Holyrood. Supporters of greater financial devolution argue it is only by making a Scottish Parliament more responsible and accountable for its financial behaviour that the Union will be preserved.

As an opponent of devolution who was willing to step forward and establish 'Think Twice' – the No No campaign in the 1997 devolution referendum – I am only too well aware that a self-financing parliament carries many risks. It is, I believe, a logical conclusion that if the Parliament is neither to disappoint Scottish patriots who ask only for a degree of home rule within the United Kingdom but feel the current formula is too weak, nor to aggravate the broader electorate because it adopts bizarre priorities built upon a seemingly endless supply of easy money, then the Holyrood parliament must be reformed and made fit for purpose. To make it more powerful *and* more accountable is, I am convinced, less of a risk than doing nothing. Financial accountability is crucial to any and every level of government in any constitutional system.

Federal systems, as in the United States, Canada and Germany, have some degree of fiscal autonomy. So does the still evolving devolved system of Spain, where provinces are able to access a range of powers such as varying certain taxes within a set range. Indeed, the Basque country already successfully operates a system much like the one that Fry *et al.* proposed for Scotland in 1988, and there we have also a clear example of a separatist threat being defused. Fiscal autonomy as such does not, therefore, predicate the particular political outcome of independence.

There are some in the Scottish Nationalist Party who believe fiscal autonomy is just another stepping-stone on the way to establishing an independent Scottish state and are therefore willing to see it promoted. There are others in the SNP, and certainly many in its wider electoral support, who would be perfectly content with a Holyrood parliament that had far greater financial powers and would settle for this over outright independence. Indeed, such a settlement would, I believe, precipitate a political realignment across the Conservative and SNP parties, as a sizeable minority of SNP politicians have no interest in establishing embassies or raising an army. There are, of course, some in the SNP who are completely against fiscal autonomy, either because they correctly identify it as a unionist threat to their ultimate goal – or because they believe that tactically they must continue to promote independence for fear of losing any understanding and sympathy for their ideal.

Despite recent opinion polls showing a higher than usual degree of support for the SNP and its policy of independence the unionist parties continue to enjoy about 60% of the public's support. Significantly, even when opinion polls show a majority of Scots supporting independence, the combined party support still lies with the unionists, suggesting that one person's independence is another person's home rule and that, for others, it is a concept that whilst maybe desirable is so far down the political agenda that it does not transfer into support of the one party that promises to deliver it.

There is a small but dedicated band of people who believe, as Welsh Secretary of State Ron Davies MP put it, that 'devolution is a process not an event'. They believe that devolution must evolve and that as more powers reside with the Scottish Parliament then so its politicians and its people will grow in self confidence and believe they are ready to take on further powers until there is nothing that the Scottish Parliament should not do.

There is a logic and rational line of thought to this but it is not impossible to challenge it. It would be a mistake to argue that there are certain responsibilities that Scots or the Scottish Parliament are not capable of handling. That is clearly nonsense.[18]

It is my contention that a Scottish Parliament can take on further powers over time but that there are certain responsibilities, such as defence, foreign relations, immigration, welfare benefits – including state pensions, trade regulations and employment law – that can benefit from economies of scale or from the natural boundaries of

Britain. Britain's trade and cultural history provide invaluable opportunities that can be exploited by a worldwide trading nation such as Scotland. The UK's influence in the United Nations – for example, on the Security Council – is the envy of many countries. Such advantages, which are not just beneficial economically in jobs and prosperity but in peace and security, should not be given up lightly. It is for these reasons – that it is essentially to Scotland's benefit that it is able to be part of the United Kingdom – that I am convinced that while, on balance, Scots would like the Holyrood parliament to have more responsibilities they also believe that pooling other government activities makes a great deal of sense. Were the Scottish Parliament to have its own Treasury and Chancellor, enjoying proper budget debates and financial scrutiny, then some SNP voters might recoil from going any further. This is not mere speculation but is supported by the attitudinal surveys carried out by Edinburgh University's Institute of Governance. These throw up some revealing preferences, which should encourage supporters of greater powers for Holyrood but disappoint hard-line unionists and nationalists.

Firstly, it is not surprising to find that half of those people who consider themselves 'Scottish not British' should support independence. What is surprising is that what might be thought of as the most unionist group, those that consider themselves 'more British than Scottish', give their largest preference to a Scottish Parliament with tax-raising powers, as in fact do those who consider themselves 'equally Scottish and British' or 'more Scottish than British'. The least popular option in all four groupings is a Scottish Parliament without tax-raising powers – a position that I would suggest we are currently heading towards, with no party advocating the use of the Tartan Tax and the Parliament re-establishing a Uniform Business Rate.

National identity by constitutional preference, 2005

Group identity	No Parliament	Holyrood without tax	Holyrood with tax	Independence
Scottish not British	7%	4%	26%	51%
More Scottish than British	14%	6%	40%	34%
Scottish and British	16%	8%	49%	20%
More British than Scottish	32%	8%	38%	19%

Percentages run across rows
[Source: Institute of Governance, University of Edinburgh]

National identity by party preference

Group identity	SNP	Labour	Lib Dem	Tory
Scottish not British	51%	31%	22%	21%
More Scottish than British	36%	35%	34%	29%
Scottish and British	9%	24%	22%	26%
More British than Scottish	2%	7%	13%	20%

Percentages run down columns
[Source: Institute of Governance, University of Edinburgh]

When the same distinct groups were asked about their party preferences it is again not surprising to see where the SNP vote might come from. But what might surprise readers is how the Conservative sympathisers are drawn nearly equally from all four categories, with the 'more British than Scottish' group the smallest, at only 20%, against those with an at least equal if not greater sense of Scottish identity. Looking at the other unionist parties suggests that their support is predominantly drawn from those who have a strong sense of Scottish identity, but this need not necessarily develop into support for full independence.

The SNP has a tendency to see support for its candidates as an endorsement for independence as a whole. But it is clear that many of those who vote for it are not believers in independence but simply want either Home Rule or a strong voice for Scotland within the Union – and believe that the SNP might provide that. There are of course real practical difficulties for the SNP with the policy of fiscal autonomy. Given the leftist collectivist consensus in Scottish politics, and especially in the SNP, the inability of first Andrew Wilson and then Jim Mather to convert their colleagues to market economics does not send encouraging messages to those who might want to support fiscal autonomy, never mind full separation from the UK.

Whilst Andrew Wilson made many speeches on the Mound arguing for lower corporation tax, this was in stark contrast to the other spokesmen who called daily for higher public expenditure and displayed naked hostility towards any private sector involvement in the running of public services. Jim Mather has brought the same routine to the new Holyrood chamber, only to be more humiliatingly rebuffed as we have all witnessed anti-business policies on planning laws and New Year's Day trading being adopted by the SNP, contrary to Mather's pro-business pronouncements.

Of course, any SNP argument for fiscal autonomy is always ultimately unconvincing, as the opportunity to deliver such a system will only present itself when a Westminster government is convinced it should introduce it. Were the SNP ever to be in a position to instigate fiscal autonomy – through a referendum or by having a majority of members in either parliament – it would at that instant also have the ability to go for the jugular and introduce independence. Why settle for only GBH when it could get away with murder?

All then that SNP agitation for fiscal autonomy does is damage the prospects of it ever coming about. Cynics and conspiracy theorists might think that that's exactly why the SNP promotes it – the policy makes them sound moderate and reasonable, as opposed to rabid and extreme, whilst persuading some unionists that it is a slippery slope that should be resisted.

Fiscal autonomy – the challenges

There are a great many problems, real or imagined, that would face the introduction of some form of fiscal autonomy at the Scottish Parliament. Some occur naturally, some are the invention of political opponents and some are economic illusions. The most significant challenges are the questions of rising taxes, electoral ambivalence, financial deficit or surplus, and union dividend or premium.

Rising taxes?

The first and most obvious difficulty that could stem from a Parliament required to raise its own money would be if Scotland's politicians behaved like children set loose in a sweetie shop and thought they could endlessly raise taxes. In my opinion, such is the general level of taxation achieved by Gordon Brown that the pressures are more likely to be the other way round.

It is worth remarking here that Scottish politicians already are in a sweetie shop, able to consume as many sherbet lemons as their stomachs can take – without paying. Remember, they do not put their hands in their pockets for the spending decisions they make; they simply have to second-guess which sweets the public, and especially their friends, might like and then dish them out. They do not even need to put their hands into the taxpayers' pockets – Uncle Gordon at the Treasury already does that for them. There is no pain, they don't get their knuckles rapped, nor does the gorging on sweets give them a sore tummy.

If Scotland were to increase its personal taxes compared with its competitors in the global market in general, and with England in particular, it would see its economy suffer. As a general observation, in the global economy smaller and weaker economies adjacent to larger and stronger economies can only follow the path of lower taxes and deregulation in order to established a competitive advantage. A fiscally autonomous or fully independent Scotland would be under just such pressure. While Scotland has some high performing economic sectors, such as financial services and higher education, they both, like so many of Scotland's enterprises, rely heavily on the quality of their personnel. Raising income tax or indirect taxes that raise the cost of living would make Scotland a far less attractive location for international talent and encourage more of our own best minds to look for work elsewhere. As well as losing the tax revenue of high earners, without access to the best minds the performance of Scottish businesses could be expected to decline, causing profits to falter and economic perform-ance to be poor – also affecting tax revenues. Raising personal taxes would be an own goal for Scotland.

Some politicians might try and avoid public opposition or a brain drain by raising corporate taxes; however, similar obstacles would exist for this approach. There is already a clamour for lower corporation tax in Northern Ireland due to the far lower corporate tax rate in the neighbouring Republic of Ireland and this has created a demand – even from Labour members and apparently the First Minister – that Scotland would have to have a similar corporation tax regime as the Province. Clearly tax competition is a powerful force in directing public policy. The growing number of European countries with low corporate taxes as well as flat personal taxes would make such an anti-business policy unlikely to succeed.

In Scotland we are often asked to admire the nearby example of Ireland. Ireland is a country not of high taxes, but of low corporate taxes. It took Ireland some sixty years of poverty to learn this lesson but since then its economy has shown impressive economic growth. Sweden is often cited as a high tax and high public spending economy that still achieves impressive economic growth. What few notice is that it has relatively low business taxes and costs so that its economy is dynamic, while the taxes are concentrated on earnings and consumption. Even this model may now change, faced as Scandinavia is with low flat tax economies across the Baltic Sea. In a Scotland of high corporate taxes, capital, which is now highly mobile, would shift away very quickly to more welcoming locations. The effect on property values from such capital flight or the departure of high earners would be deflationary and the impact on our property-based economy would undoubtedly be damaging. Inward investors, be they in manufacturing, financial services or distribution, would hardly be attracted with promises that we intend to tax them more than our competitors would. Such is the huge scale of the public sector in Scotland that large private sector employers are easily identifiable and MSPs would soon be aware of a declining economy. I well remember the horror on the faces of Labour MSPs at the time of the closures of many electronic manufacturing plants in 2000 as they feared a traditional Labour economic crisis. Raising corporate taxes would be another own goal for Scotland.

I'm not saying tax rises would be impossible: I'm simply suggesting they would very quickly become counter-productive and create a political demand for tax cuts, causing casualties amongst those parties that had introduced the original tax hikes.

Scottish business appears to be divided on the issue, with the Scottish CBI and Chambers of Commerce voicing opposition, while a 2001 opinion survey of business leaders showed support of 84% in favour. The past experience of many in our business community is that collectivist politicians have previously seen the private sector as a soft target, using non-domestic rates in particular to reap financial dividends at no political cost. The business rate can of course go down as well as up and business would be less concerned about fiscal autonomy if higher costs instead became competitive advantages. Would Scotland prefer to start a game with two own goals or, by cutting its own taxes, have a two-goal start?

Electoral ambivalence?

The second challenge would come if, despite the influence of tax competition, the Scottish public felt less threatened by higher taxes or less attracted to lower taxes because there were insufficient numbers of them paying personal taxes compared to the rest of the United Kingdom. In such circumstances we could expect the general level of taxation to defy gravity and rise. The argument that Scottish politicians will be tempted to raise personal taxes because Scotland's tax base relative to the UK's electorate is small has been made often in the past. It seemed a believable and credible argument, one that I was willing to accept, but new evidence from research carried out by my own parliamentary staff tells a completely different story. The deviation has, over the last ten years, actually been slight to the point of being irrelevant and in the last two years the proportion of Scots paying income tax has actually been higher than that in the UK – 65.34% in Scotland against 64.6% in the UK in 2005–06.[19]

Another version of the same argument alleges that Scotland is a benefit junkie and therefore the number of people economically active[20] and interested in taxes is smaller and consequently will not be concerned if taxes rise. Looking at the proportion of the Scottish workforce to determine the proportion of economically active adults paying income tax shows the same trend – a relatively narrow gap, with the Scottish percentage becoming higher than the UK's in recent years. The proportion of those in employment paying taxes is 98.61% in Scotland against 95.96% in the UK in 2006–07. The evidence provides no grounds to believe that Scots will behave any differently when it comes to making decisions about whether or not to vote for parties that will raise taxes. If anything, we might expect Scots voters to be more concerned that personal taxes should fall rather than rise.

Finally, it is said that because there is a greater proportion of Scots working in the public sector than there is in the UK that any increase in personal taxes will be neutralised by the Scottish Executive compensating its workers by increasing their pay. Such cynicism of the 'bad drives out good' school can only be countered by optimism that good drives out bad. It takes no account of the fact that one of the motivations behind introducing fiscal autonomy is to adjust the balance between public and private sectors in the private sector's favour. It takes no account of how fiscal autonomy would work and the checks that would be put in place – such as Treasury rules – and the work of the Parliament's finance and audit committees that highlight the poor value for money that Executive pay bargaining has delivered. It is the argument of futility: nothing can be changed for the better so why bother? I reject this pessimism and note that those unionists advocating fiscal autonomy are without exception those that believe in sound finances, value for money, small government and low taxes. If they can convince the public that they are right then it will be because they will be saying Scotland must change and we must be self-sufficient in our public spending – Scotland will not be going into this with its eyes shut.

Also worthy of consideration is the recent record of pay settlements for GPs, consultants, teachers and others, which have been hugely expensive but then failed to demonstrate any productivity gains. The Auditor General, the Audit and Finance Committees, Her Majesty's Inspectorate of Education, and others have all produced highly critical reports that will make it far more difficult to award such pushover pay deals in the future.

Deficit or surplus?

A third challenge is the question of Scotland's budget deficit or surplus. But this in reality shows the strength of full fiscal autonomy as a unionist, not a separatist, policy. The question of whether Scotland can pay its way as an independent country is an interesting and important one which commentators have argued about for years without ever coming to a certain conclusion; though, following the explosion in public spending under Gordon Brown, the balance of the evidence is currently against the separatists. Whether Scotland can pay its way is, however, not the point at issue if we are discussing devolution in general and fiscal autonomy in particular. In these more limited cases the question is whether the *devolved* services can be financed – an answer that would appear to be an obvious yes if the annual Government Expenditure and Revenue in Scotland (GERS)[21] statistical document is to be believed.

The ability of Scotland to meet its Scottish Executive spending is not in question – the arguments about funding the remaining non-devolved expenditure can therefore be addressed separately (with or without all or some of the oil revenues). Fiscal autonomy offers a way out of this dead end because the devolved services account for just under half of all public expenditure in Scotland, £25.8 billion out of £47.7 billion (2004/05 figures).

Scottish public spending and revenue 2000/01–2004/05

Year	2000–01	2001–02	2002–03	2003–04	2004–05
A Tax revenues excluding Oil	30.386	31.186	31.601	33.972	36.439
Oil revenues	4.3	5.2	4.9	4.3	5.2
B Tax revenues including Oil	34.686	36.386	36.501	38.272	41.639
C Total managed expenditure	*35.641*	*38.868*	*41.436*	*45.226*	*47.662*
D Of which devolved Executive spending	17.6	19.607	22.373	24.803	25.819
(Deficit)/Surplus (A–C) without oil	(5.255)	(7.682)	(9.835)	(11.254)	(11.223)
(Deficit)/Surplus (B– C) with oil	(0.955)	(2.482)	(4.935)	(6.954)	(6.023)
Revenue less Executive spending (A– D)	12.786	11.579	9.228	9.169	10.620

[Source: Government Expenditure and Revenue in Scotland]

It is plain as a pikestaff that this sum of £25.8 billion can be financed out of the revenue of £36.4 billion (excluding oil) raised in Scotland. People may dispute the accuracy of the revenues but I have not heard anyone say they are so low as not to cover devolved spending. Indeed, complaints from nationalists are that the revenues are underestimated. Using these figures would leave a balance of £10.6 billion, £15.8 billion if all the oil revenues are included. This would represent the precept, as it was called by Fry *et al.*, going to London to meet our share of the common expenses of the United Kingdom – which according to the 2004/05 figures would have been £21.9 billion for Scotland. That would suggest leaving a shortfall of £6.1 billion – a gap that in practice arises from nothing more than national accounting conventions – but at least the UK's subsidy to Scotland becomes explicit. At less than one per cent of the UK's gross domestic product it is, I suggest, a very small price for keeping the Union together.

The figure may go up or down, although the changes in financial discipline and pressures to reign back per capita spending with a reformed Barnett Formula, plus the possibility of increased tax revenues from a more dynamic economy, could significantly narrow the gap and in good times possibly lead to a surplus being paid rather than a subsidy received. A new Barnett Formula would have to take account of this latter possibility too. Of course, nationalists would argue that if Scotland can send a positive precept and therefore stand financially alone then it should opt for independence altogether. I would simply argue that there are many benefits to the Union and having an insurance policy that smoothes out economic shocks and secures public services in fallow years but expects a modest premium in productive years is in fact a highly attractive bargain worth agreeing to. Placed alongside the UK's annual membership fee of the European Union of £11 billion and net cost of between £17 and £40 billion,[22] a variance either way of £6 billion between Scotland and the UK must surely be irresistible to both parties?

Union dividend or premium?

The final challenge is the political question for unionists; if Scotland can be seen to benefit and do well from such fiscal autonomy what would there be to stop it from striking out for full independence? It is a good question but the answer lies in the supposition that the Union is essentially an economic one. There have been many decades when England subsidised the standard of living of Scotland and many decades when the reverse was true. If the Union is defended merely as a source of subsidy the separatists will simply wait until the day when Scotland is in surplus and say we don't need England any more. Indeed they make that claim already about most of the 1980s – although it is hotly disputed. If we defend the Union purely on the basis of a subsidy received – what has been termed part of a 'Union Dividend' – then the argument will fall if our prosperity grows and we need to contribute to help less well-off parts of the United Kingdom. The Union provides insurance cover for harder economic times to all parts of the United Kingdom: when we are in sunnier climes we should be prepared to help poorer regions of the UK – what we might term the 'Union Premium'. Only if we bring this aspect into the economic debate will the concept of the Union be fully understood, and our obligations recognised and honoured if called upon. I don't want Scotland to be a subsidy junky relying on England or the rest of the UK, and I don't want Scotland to be a dependency culture. I want to see Scotland prosper and grow and become the strongest economic unit in the United Kingdom, with even greater influence within the political relationship.

Politicians who focus only on the economic aspects of the Union do it a great disservice but, as it is not the main topic of this tract, I will simply say that the cultural, historical and strategic defence of the Union must become more pronounced. Unionism must be seen to be warm and outward looking, not cold and selfish, or it will fail. The Union is like a marriage – there may be occasional quarrels over money, but they need not end in divorce.

The benefits

Having considered the range of obstacles that fiscal autonomy would face, the other side of the equation to be considered is the benefits such a system might offer that would make it worthwhile: principally, real tax cuts and political accountability.

The first benefit is that it will be possible for Scottish politicians to genuinely offer tax cuts knowing that higher tax revenues accruing from increased productivity or consumption would come to a Scottish Treasury and not go to Westminster. The economic and political debate in Scotland can then mature because both sides to the public spending equation can be put. Generally speaking, the countries with the lowest taxes achieve the highest growth.

Countries that overtax themselves suffer lower growth. Of course, a trade-off can be attempted between tax and growth, but on the whole the best way to achieve high revenues is to achieve high growth – the revenues then come not through raising rates of tax but through greater output. To raise rates of tax in a country of lower output, like Scotland, certainly seems the best way to depress rather than increase growth. In other words, high taxes make us all poorer, and less capable of tackling the social problems they are meant to solve. From the perspective of supporters of small government, the prevailing culture of public spending needs to be broken. This will not happen so long as Scottish politicians are free to put their hands in the pockets of the English taxpayer.

The second benefit is that as taxation and spending become more transparent so Scottish politicians will become more accountable to the electorate through debate, scrutiny and media coverage of the financial options that would now be real and visible.

The main political ramification of such transparency is likely to be a more realistic approach to what a Scottish Government can afford to spend in the future and greater honesty from politicians. The incentives that I have mentioned earlier would now begin to work in favour of making savings and reducing public spending so that the tax take could be lower. Efficiency gains would have real meaning, would have to be realised, and savings could actually be returned to the taxpayer. Finally, if their politicians fail them, the people of Scotland will be informed enough to take matters into their own hands, to demand tax-cuts and mobilise political forces to produce them through action on programmes of public expenditure.

How can we deliver fiscal autonomy?

How then might fiscal autonomy work? Firstly, the Scottish Executive needs to establish a Treasury Department out of its current finance responsibilities. This is badly needed already and even without fiscal autonomy would still be of immense benefit to the control and prioritisation of public spending in Scotland. Jim and Margaret Cuthbert have already written on the subject[23], while

Professor Alan Peacock made a similar call for a Treasury department in the Policy Institute paper *What Future for Scotland?*[24] – so I shall not labour the point. Creating a Scottish Treasury that will put its own internal disciplines on departmental spending, and can point to the costs of policies when others in government only want to consider the benefits, is a prerequisite for a prudent public sector which allows enough room for the private sector to create the wealth that it lives off.

Over the last couple of years there have thankfully been a number of academic papers that have sought to study the various options in some detail. Initial work by Professor Ronald MacDonald and Professor Paul Hallwood explained how fiscal federalism could be introduced by assigning certain taxes collected by Westminster to the Scottish Parliament. This would be an advance from the Barnett Formula, as it would mean that spending was more closely related to tax revenues, even if they were not entirely set by Holyrood.[25] The key taxes they identified were income tax, VAT and corporation tax. Further work by MacDonald and Hallwood[26] then explored how fiscal autonomy could work by making the Scottish Parliament responsible for raising every pound it spent by collecting its own taxes – possibly paying a precept for defence etc. along the lines suggested by Fry. In the same paper they also discussed 'full fiscal autonomy', which was to all intents and purposes independence. This paper was especially important as it brought some much needed rigour to the debate. Up until then politicians had been bandying all sorts of names for fiscal devolution and the loose use of language had meant some politicians sounded vague or were talking at cross-purposes, I suspect intentionally so.

MacDonald and Hallwood had also undertaken a useful review of other papers on related subjects, including the ability of fiscal devolution to encourage growth, and pointed to the work of Stansel[27] to show a positive relationship between fiscal decentralisation and economic growth and the work of Lee and Gordon[28], which suggests that faster rates of economic growth follow corporation tax cuts. They state, 'There is now compelling empirical support for a link between the ability to change taxes on labour and capital and the efficiency with which resources are allocated within a country or region.' Also of importance is their consideration of how a Scottish government within the UK could finance a budget deficit through Scottish Treasury securities. They point out that borrowing, 'would not be entirely at the discretion of the Scottish government because of the need to maintain consistency in the budget stance of the UK as a whole. A stability pact limiting the size [of borrowing] would be needed.' Finally, they raise the advantages of Scotland enjoying a common currency with the rest of the United Kingdom, which – even were Scotland to become independent – they argue is beneficial. While Scotland remains in the UK having a different currency is simply not an issue and gives a fiscally autonomous Scotland some protection from asymmetrical economic shocks that arise within the Union.

Encouraging debate to the full, the Policy Institute then followed the MacDonald and Hallwood arguments with a paper by Professor Sir Donald MacKay and Professor David Bell which, while arguing cogently against the high public spending levels in Scotland, warned against fiscal autonomy as it risked independence.[29] One argument MacKay and Bell proffered was: 'In Scotland's case full fiscal autonomy would mean huge reductions in Scottish public expenditure unless North Sea oil and gas revenues were to accrue to the Scottish exchequer and this would create further economic and political tensions.' While there was substantial economic evidence presented to back up their case regarding poorer economic growth stemming from high public spending there was no political evidence given to support the argument of increased political tension. I have no doubt that the Treasury in London would want to resist foregoing its oil and gas revenues (of which as much as 10% comes from English waters); however, if the decision had been taken to replace Barnett by fiscal autonomy it would be a political decision taken at the highest level, with the agreement of Cabinet. That is because fiscal autonomy is primarily a political question, not an economic one. Although it is about finances the greatest issue is the political instability that the current settlement represents. This is what will ultimately bring about the impetus to deliver change. It would therefore not be in the Treasury's interest, or in that of its boss the Chancellor, to introduce a new system that was unstable and would quickly need to be revisited. Political will is what would determine that the oil revenues, possibly 90% of them, should accrue to Scotland. I have tested this hypothetical situation on a number of leading Tory politicians in England and have never found the prospect of Scotland retaining the oil revenues to be anything resembling a difficulty. Although it is unusual for taxes accruing from natural resources to be allocated to regional parliaments in countries that have federal arrangements, such is the totemic significance that 'Scotland's oil' has gained since the 1970s, not including it in any new financial arrangement would only put the Union at risk. As this would be counter to one of the main reasons for securing new arrangements, I do not accept tension is a serious proposition.

For myself I do not believe it is necessary at this stage to take a hard line that all taxes should be collected in Scotland, and that all should be set at different rates from those pertaining in the rest of the UK. All that is required at this stage is to accept the principle of the Scottish Parliament covering all or most of its costs by itself. While fiscal autonomy has been defined by MacDonald and Hallwood as being separate from fiscal federalism, because the former is about levying and varying taxes at Holyrood and the latter is about assigning them from Westminster, there is also the likelihood that fiscal autonomy might lead to arrangements that use some of the benefits of scale that the Union can bring. There is no need for unionist politicians to be dogmatic about this issue.

The testing of devolution

It is beyond argument that devolution has greatly disappointed the Scottish public. After its first four-year term less than half, a humiliating 49% of those entitled to vote, turned out in the election of May 2003. Much was said in the eighteen years of Conservative government about how life could be so much better if only we had our own Scottish Parliament. Inflated claims about its low running costs and its ability to help Scotland's economy, culture and environment were made during the referendum campaign of 1997.

To blame the Parliament for the disenchantment is, however, going too far. The failures are political not institutional and the blame lies, therefore, with the ruling political consensus – indeed many of the successes could have been delivered without devolution by simply changing the Westminster government, a change that did eventually come. It is important to remember, however, that the SNP, as the main opposition party, is also signed up to the social democrat model that advocates more spend and waste policies. The SNP is seen as the main opposition party and so support for the SNP does not mean there is wholesale opposition to the institution or that independence is desired.

Before the elections of May 2003 we had the untimely death of Donald Dewar, the repeal of Section 2A against the clear will of the Scottish people and a variety of close political shaves over tuition fees, care for the elderly and compensation for fishermen, as well as the replacement of Henry McLeish by Jack McConnell. None of the foregoing political tests had, however, any significant constitutional implications and, although bruised, the Parliament has come through intact. I do not accept, however, that unionists should sleep easy at night, safe in the comfort that devolution is not the unbalanced destabilising constitutional nightmare that they feared, for the unspoken truth is that Holyrood has not yet faced a genuine constitutional crisis or the political exploitation that usually follows such a crisis.

How well the Scottish Parliament would come out of a constitutional crisis, what opportunities political parties would have to exploit such a crisis and how the public might therefore respond would determine if the current institutional model we have is a friend or enemy of the Union. By considering what scenario a financially self-reliant Scottish Parliament might deliver we shall then be able to consider if greater powers would be a reinforcement or weakening of the current arrangements as they affect the Union.

Firstly then, we should look at a number of threats that the current Scottish Parliament could face and what might arise out of them. Michael Forsyth famously warned that 'a Scottish Parliament is not just for Christmas – it's for life.'[30] Amongst a number of problems he could have been alluding to was a constitutional disagreement between Westminster and Holyrood. The fear for unionists would be that, were the Scottish public to be behind the Scottish Parliament and against Westminster, then the more likely result would be a gradual political deterioration leading to the break up of the United Kingdom rather than Holyrood's abolition.

It is not difficult to conceive of a number of situations where the Edinburgh and London institutions could have different ruling parties.

At Holyrood the permutations are greater and more complex and, because of its proportional representation voting, it will always involve two parties. Labour could continue with the support of the Liberal Democrats; Labour could rely upon the Conservatives; the SNP could forge a coalition with the Liberal Democrats; although currently unlikely, the SNP could rely upon Conservative support; and almost inconceivable would be a grand coalition between the SNP and Labour. Of course a ruling coalition may require three party groups to achieve the sixty-five MSP overall majority required and this would most likely come from the Greens. The first eight years of the new devolved parliament have enjoyed Labour-led administrations but it is not too much a stretch of the imagination to expect that at some point in, say, the next eight years, the Scottish electorate will choose a government that does not have Labour as a member.

Westminster is likely to have one of only three permutations; a Labour Government, a Conservative Government or a hung parliament with a minority government of either of those parties supported by the Liberal Democrats. While it may still be treated with disbelief by some, it is certainly possible that the Conservatives will return to power at Westminster at the next, or next again, general election, either as a minority or coalition government – or even in outright power (although the arithmetical challenge for the latter outcome remains a considerable one). Whatever the scenario, there is every prospect that Labour will be out of power in one or both of the parliaments in the next twelve years.

As to what political reactions such scenarios might throw up it is not the subject of this book to speculate at length so I shall restrict myself to two basic assumptions. The first is where an SNP-led Scottish Executive is faced with either a Labour or Conservative-led administration at Westminster with Labour in opposition in Edinburgh. The second is where Labour remains in power in Edinburgh but the Conservatives have taken the reins of authority in London.

In the first scenario, with the SNP in control in Edinburgh, whichever party was in power in London would be immaterial to Labour's behaviour as an opposition party at Holyrood trying to regain mass appeal.[31] This is wholly different from the situation currently existing, because being in opposition would place Labour in Scotland under new strains and tensions that would often require it to be *more* patriotic than the SNP. Meanwhile, an SNP-led administration would seek to capitalise on every institutional disagreement, attempting to push a wedge deeper and deeper between Scotland and the rest of the United Kingdom. Labour would quickly find itself in a marathon four-year competition with the nationalists to define and represent what Scotland's best interests were. In such circumstances, even a Labour Government at Whitehall would find Labour MSPs willing to criticise and speak out against it, just as local councillors are often left with little option but to criticise their own party in central government when their political survival is at stake.

In the second scenario, with Labour still in power in Scotland but faced with a Conservative UK Government there would undoubtedly be occasions, especially in financial and economic policy, where Labour would begin to play the small 'n' nationalist card, partly to avoid being outflanked by the SNP and partly because it would marginalise the Scottish Tories. In other words, Labour would revert to type, with the Liberal Democrats following in its wake. The constitutional arrangements on which the Parliament has been built would be undermined in the same way as when they were pre-devolution, using the arguments of grievance, just as Britain's unitary structures were challenged throughout the years of Margaret Thatcher and John Major. Indeed, it is hard to conceive of a scenario where Westminster and its governments, of whichever parties, would not be blamed for the perceived difficulties that Scotland might be presented with.

If asymmetric devolution is to work properly it cannot require that Labour is forever in government in both Westminster and Holyrood; it must be robust enough to survive governments of different views.

These different views will often find expression in higher or lower levels of public spending, either in aggregate terms, where one party wants to roll back the state while a second party wants to roll it forward, or in particular terms, where one party wants to spend more on the police or on roads while a second party wants to spend more on education or health. Under devolution we are perfectly entitled to make our own decisions about these things, but it will become increasingly more difficult to squeeze them all within one fiscal system. If devolved government is moving in one direction and central government in another, the economic, political and constitutional forces will be pulling apart. Surely then the financial structure of Scottish government must be reviewed by unionists so that a system can be put in place that does not require like-minded parties to form the government in both parliaments. A system that allows the Scottish Parliament to make its own funding decisions based upon the parties' democratic mandates, without having to ask taxpayers from the rest of the United Kingdom to subsidise these choices, would make it difficult to blame London, Westminster or 'the English' – while it would also neutralise tensions in England about Scotland's high per capita spending and make 'English votes for English Laws' a credible solution to the West Lothian question.

I have no doubts that fiscal autonomy is a high-risk strategy, but so too is preserving the status quo. The risk to the maintenance of the Union started when the principle of asymmetric devolution was conceded for electoral advantage by Labour and was compounded by introducing a model that was entirely to the benefit of its progenitors – the Labour and Liberal Democrat parties – rather than providing a structure that would offer stability for the long term.

Labour's devolution settlement is real, so we must face up to the difficulties ahead to ensure the edifice holds together. To do nothing and leave the current arrangements as they are is to invite a political crisis that could be disastrous for Scotland and the Union.

NOTES

1. The formula was never presented to Parliament but was agreed by Jim Callaghan's Cabinet and later revealed in a Parliamentary answer by Tory Scottish Secretary George Younger.
2. Professors Ronald MacDonald and Paul Hallwood have called this journey to fiscal autonomy the 'Glide Path'. See P. Hallwood and R. MacDonald: *The Economic Case For Fiscal Autonomy: with or without independence*, Policy Institute, Edinburgh, 2006.
3. The percentages used for the Scottish block grant have been: Goschen Formula 13.75% (1888), Barnett Formula 11.76% (1978), Adjusted Barnett Formula 10.23% (2002). See D. Bell: *Research Paper 01/108, The Barnett Formula*, House of Commons Library, London, 2001.
4. On the Tory floor of the MSP offices we christened it 'Barnett Plus' because if English public spending was slowing and Scottish spending wasn't it could only mean that our share of spending per head of population would increase.
5. With political manipulation of the formula by Conservative Treasury Ministers in the past (to avoid painful cuts in public spending, of course) and such a burgeoning budget now, any convergence over the last thirty years is not visible to the untrained eye.
6. Bell, *Research Paper 01/108*.
7.

UK Population figures

	1976	1981	1991	2001
Scotland	5,233,000	5,180,000	5,083,300	5,064,200
England	46,660,000	46,821,000	47,875,000	49,449,700
UK	56,216,000	56,357,000	57,438,700	59,113,500

[Source: ONS estimates based on Census data (1976 based on ONS mid decade estimate)]

8. Margaret Thatcher became the first Prime Minister since the second Earl of Liverpool to lead a party to three successive election victories.
9. Q. Jardine, R. Leckie, B. Meek and S. Stevenson: *Unlocking the Future* (ed. M. Fry), The Conservative Constitutional Reform Forum, Edinburgh, 1998.
10. The Tuesday Club is a political dining club founded in 1996 by the author, Struan Stevenson and Michael Fry to encourage new policy ideas for a Conservative revival in Scotland. It has no corporate view.
11. M. Fraser, M. Fry and P. Smaill: *Full Fiscal Freedom for the Scottish Parliament*, The Tuesday Club, Edinburgh, 1998.
12. Gerald Warner, *Scotland on Sunday*, 1 September 2002.
13. Gerald Warner, *Scotland on Sunday*, 7 December 2003.
14. Gerald Warner, *Scotland on Sunday*, 29 October 2006.
15. 'There would be no barbed wire or collapse . . .' P. Fraser, *The Sunday Times*, 3 December 2006.

16. D. Steel (ed.): *The Steel Commission: Moving to Federalism – A New Settlement for Scotland*, Scottish Liberal Democrat Party, Edinburgh, 2005.
17. A. Massie: 'Change is the best option for the Status Quo', in *Scotland's Ten Tomorrows, The Devolution Crisis and how to solve it* (ed. B. Jamieson), Continuum, London, 2006.
18. Since the days of Henry Dundas in the eighteenth century Scots have run all the great ministries and departments of state at Whitehall. What is important is not Scotland's size but the socio-economic policies and regulatory structures that allow a small country to meet its people's desires.
19.

Voters who pay income tax: Scotland compared to UK

Year	UK electorate	UK income tax payers	Scottish electorate	Scottish income tax payers	% of UK voters paying IT	% of Scottish voters paying IT
1997–1998	43,846,000	26,200,000	3,984,406	2,370,000	59.75%	59.48%
1999–2000	44,692,299	27,008,000	4,027,433	2,270,000	60.40%	56.36%
2001–2002	44,695,764	29,000,000	3,966,801	2,450,000	64.88%	61.76%
2003–2004	44,118,053	30,400,000	3,857,997	2,470,000	68.91%	64.00%
2005–2006	44,944,109	29,040,000	3,887,464	2,540,000	64.60%	65.34%

Economically active who pay income tax: Scotland compared to UK

Year	Economically active UK (millions)	UK income tax payers	Economically active Scotland (millions)	Scottish income tax payers	% of Scottish workforce paying IT	% of UK workforce paying IT
1997–1998	28.497	26,200,000	2.481	2,370,000	95.53%	91.94%
1999–2000	28.987	27,008,000	2.474	2,270,000	91.75%	93.17%
2001–2002	29.297	29,000,000	2.510	2,450,000	97.60%	98.99%
2003–2004	29.712	30,400,000	2.543	2,470,000	97.13%	100.0%
2005–2006	30.31	29,040,000	2.603	2,540,000	97.58%	95.80%

[Source: National Statistics (http://www.statistics.gov.uk)]

20. 'Economically Active' is defined in the Labour Survey as 'people who are aged 16 and over who are either in employment or are unemployed'. Many people not in employment but with pensions or income from investments also pay income tax. In addition some people in employment may not be defined as part of the potential work force if they are older than the conventional retirement age.

21. The criticism of GERS by the SNP politicians is disingenuous, for they cannot say that the figures are wrong and then argue that the same figures show that Labour is damaging the Scottish economy. GERS can be used for one argument or the other, but not both.
22. I. Milne: *A Cost Too Far: An Analysis of the Net Economic Costs and Benefits for the UK of EU Membership*, Civitas, London, 2004.
23. J. and M. Cuthbert: 'Opposing but not imposing', *Scottish Left Review* 24, September/October 2004.
24. A. Peacock *et al.*: *What Future for Scotland? – Policy Options for Devolution*, Policy Institute, Edinburgh, 2003.
25. P. Hallwood, Paul and R. MacDonald: *The Economic Case for Fiscal Federalism in Scotland*, The Allander Series, Essay 8, 2004.
26. Hallwood and MacDonald (2006) *The Economic Case For Fiscal Autonomy*.
27. D. Stansel: 'Local decentralization and economic growth: A cross-sectional examination of US metropolitan areas', *Journal of Urban Economics* 57, 2005, pp. 55–72.
28. Y. Lee and R.H. Gordon: 'Tax structure and economic growth', *Journal of Public Economics* 89, 2005, pp. 1027–43.
29. Sir Donald Mackay and David Bell: *The Political Economy of Devolution*, Policy Institute, Edinburgh, 2006.
30. Michael Forsyth, *World at One*, BBC Radio 4, 10 February 1997.
31. The behaviour of the Scottish Labour party after every election defeat of 1979, 1983, 1987 and 1992 became more and more stridently nationalist.

Chapter 3

TAXING BUSINESS

'Government's view of the economy could be summed up in a few short phrases: If it moves, tax it. If it keeps moving, regulate it. And if it stops moving, subsidise it.'
– RONALD REAGAN

One of the central arguments put in favour of fiscal autonomy by both unionists and nationalists is that it would allow the Scottish Parliament to use fiscal policy – the setting of tax rates – to create a more dynamic Scottish economy to deliver higher economic growth. A number of international studies show lower taxes stimulate growth as business can reinvest more profit in more jobs and increased development spending.[1] There is also a great deal of evidence to show that such fiscal policies can help countries, even those with no natural resources or a skilled workforce, to achieve highly impressive economic growth. Scotland does not have such disadvantages but it is, in respect of some of its economic activity, far from some of its markets or without the economies of scale that would help drive costs of delivery or production down. Tax rates are not the whole story for Scotland's comparatively poorer performance. There has also in Scotland, I believe, thanks to decades of welfarism and our own brand of Calvinist collectivism, been engendered a significant cultural difficulty with business success, entrepreneurial endeavour and the idea of profit making.

I have never understood why profit is a dirty word for so many people in Scotland. Such people should try reading the business pages of papers and replacing the word profit with the word loss and then consider the impact on our economy. No investment in jobs where they are needed, no bonuses for staff reward, no dividends for our pension funds – and crucially no taxes to pay for public services. Although the public sector pays taxes (income taxes from employees and various property and consumption taxes), it does not do this by trading at a profit by, say, covering its costs in charges. It is almost completely financed by extracting taxes, with the full force of law behind it. In other words, it is the private sector, both personal and business, that in a competitive market and without the advantage of legal coercion, is able to add financial value to more than cover its operating costs, and thus pay through its taxes for the public sector *and the taxes it pays.*

It is more profits that Scotland needs, more burgeoning banks like the Royal Bank of Scotland and bellicose brewers like Scottish and Newcastle – or the future for our country will be the bleak socialist utopia that was East Germany on a wet Wednesday in winter.

Business tax cuts may be able to alleviate comparative disadvantages by providing new advantages for Scottish companies; they cannot, however, change the cultural disdain and misunderstanding that Scottish business or its trailblazers so often encounter. There is an anti-business culture in many parts of Scotland, or at least an ambivalence, making the choice to go into commerce more difficult, if not brave. It is so much easier to seek employment in the expanding public sector with relative job security and favourable pay and pensions than to take the initiative and establish a new venture, where the rewards may be greater but the environment is far riskier.

The statistics bear this out. Scotland's business birth rate, an issue of great concern to Scottish Enterprise and therefore a focus of much effort by the agency over the years, stubbornly refuses to come close to the UK average. Just as worrying is the high mortality rate of new Scottish ventures, again suggesting that Scotland's business climate is poor compared to the rest of the UK.[2] The

Executive's own figures on business start-ups show that, with a VAT registration rate that was 26% below the UK average in 2002, Scotland was ninth out of twelve UK regions. According to the Executive's data on small and medium-sized enterprises becoming larger companies, in 2004 Scotland had only twelve firms with value added figures of between £250 million and £1 billion, which represents about 5% of the total of 221 firms of that size in the UK.

The Executive talks about investing in a smart successful Scotland but businesses make the best investment decisions for themselves. Government ministers and their advisors looking out of their windows in Victoria Quay are no better able to predict the needs of businesses they can see with their own eyes in Leith than Scottish Enterprise consultants are able to predict the needs of the aggregate of all businesses across Scotland. Breaking business down into sectors, disciplines, markets, futures and so on still cannot overcome the fact that each business is different and will require to make its own multifarious choices at a variety of levels. Central or local economic planning cannot second-guess these choices and averaging them off to try and offer the best common denominator is doomed to fail. That's why, for example, we have so many shortages in skills at the moment. Economic planning is the cause of shortages or surpluses even when it is run well; more economic planning will not cure the problems business face – it will only make matters worse.

In this chapter I shall look at what might be done in Scotland if it had the power to manage the taxes that affect business and trade. There are two candidates: non-domestic or business rates and corporation tax. I will discuss business rates first, because the Scottish Parliament *already* has the power to vary, and indeed abolish or add to, the business rates in Scotland. It is collected in Scotland, and paid to the Treasury as the banker that then returns it on top of the Scottish Executive's block grant.

Business rates

Back in the 1970s and 1980s a succession of Labour-run councils used business rates as a cash cow to pay for municipal profligacy.

Businesses could be taxed into oblivion – and they were – for they no longer had votes. They did, however, have the ability to move, and many of them did, or simply closed down for good. Who can forget the period when Jenners paid more than Harrods or Scottish high streets were dotted with hoardings like a measles rash proclaiming: 'To Let' or 'For Sale'? The Conservatives eventually acted by introducing a universal business rate, or UBR, which after a number of years of transition meant that the Scottish rate poundage was the same as in England.

This meant that so long as the assessors' revaluations were regular enough to ensure that they were realistic reflections of the property market, the comparatively lower values in Scotland would be reflected in a lower business rates bills – delivering a more just and equitable system. Then in 1999 Labour and the Liberals came to power and, as Finance Minister seven years ago, Jack McConnell abolished the UBR by putting up the Scottish business rates poundage. For the next four years Scottish businesses faced a higher tax than their English counterparts, handing over nearly £200 million more in taxes each year just when they needed to be more competitive than English businesses. Scottish businesses were not happy and showed their concern when they complained about the higher rates in an inquiry set up by the Scottish Executive to consider the economic and regulatory landscape for manufacturers. The Scottish Manufacturing Steering Group Report[3] said:

> Not only should parity with the rest of the UK be achieved, but there should also be a study to compare the levels of local taxation with our main competitors in Europe and the OECD . . . In the longer term, business rates offer the possibility of creating a distinct competitive advantage for Scotland.

Ministers tried to argue that a revaluation of properties in England required the Scottish rate to be different so that equity was achieved, but it was a disingenuous claim. If business rates did not matter why then did Harvey Nichols extract a commitment for a business rate waiver before locating in Edinburgh? Why did the Enterprise Minister confirm in parliamentary question[4] that part of the deal struck by the Scottish Government to keep Hoover in

Cambuslang was a promise to review its business rates? Why? For no other reason than that business rates do matter, had become comparatively more expensive and are controlled in Scotland. A survey carried out by Ernst & Young[5] among director-level personnel at Scottish firms found business rates consistently ranked in the top two concerns to be addressed by government.

On two occasions I went to the Local Government Committee to try and reverse Scottish Executive policy. Interestingly, on each occasion the Scottish Nationalist on the Committee would not vote for lower business rates.

The SNP's behaviour the first time, in 2004, might be dismissed as pure party politics: I was Conservative finance spokesman and I was proposing that the 1p increase in poundage being proposed by the Executive be annulled. I would have preferred it was reduced; that, however, was not possible through the negative instrument that procedurally I was limited to. I could only halt the increase, not propose my own far lower poundage. My case was simple enough. I argued that Scotland's economic performance was not good enough in comparative terms to the rest of the UK and internationally; that the level of poundage was an important issue to business, both domestically and comparatively with the rest of the UK and Europe; that there was no need for an increase given that the revenue raised from 2003/04 was greater than expected; and that the Executive had already conceded these arguments by introducing its own small business relief scheme and then the following year freezing business rates.[6] Following my represen-tations and the minister's response and other contributions from committee members, Andrew Welsh (SNP) voted for the increase to go through along with the Labour, Liberal, Democrat and SSP members present. So much then for the SNP saying that it would cut business rates – given the opportunity to show that policy meant something its representative voted for an increase.

In the winter of 2005 Jack McConnell announced that business rates would be reduced so that the UBR was re-established. It was clearly timed to ensure that his new Liberal Democrat deputy, Nicol Stephen, could not take credit for a policy that he had first mooted in his campaign to replace Jim Wallace as its leader. In a typically shameless performance McConnell then went on to proffer the benefits that would come from reducing the rates bill. One could not help but think that if reducing business rates was such a good thing, why had the higher burden been introduced by the same man in the first place and why stop at just matching the English level, why not undercut it significantly? But there was a catch; parity was not to be achieved immediately but over a two-year period. So, in 2006 I went back to the same committee.

By now I had become an independent and the petty partisan excuse for the SNP of not accepting a Conservative motion could not lurk in the background (these motives are never admitted to but are always at work in the murky undergrowth of politics). Again due to the procedures, the consequence of my proposition if passed (a highly unlikely prospect) was that no business rates could have been collected at all, unless the Executive brought forward a new proposal and had it passed (an inconvenience but easily within its gift, as was confirmed at the meeting). My plan was to take the opportunity of the setting of the rate poundage to argue against business rates in general and to urge the Executive to at least achieve a uniform business rate in one year rather than the two it was proposing. With tongue firmly in cheek I welcomed the Executive's proposal to achieve equalisation with England by April 2007 and commended the new Liberal Democrat leader, Nicol Stephen, for prodding the Scottish Executive into action along that path. However, I suggested it was too little, too late, for Scottish firms had already paid some £838 million more than their English counterparts since the Executive began setting the business rate at a consistently higher poundage.

George Lyon, the Liberal Democrat deputy minister for finance managed to keep a straight face when he replied that the Executive had listened to business and how business rates 'can impact on their profitability and they have argued for a level playing field with their competitors south of the border'. Keeping his straight face, he then repudiated the arguments of Andy Kerr and Jack McConnell from the previous six years when he stated his proposal, 'not only equalises the poundage but also delivers a significant competitive advantage to Scottish businesses because valuations in Scotland tend to be lower than those in England and Wales. Therefore, equalisation of the poundage rate will deliver competitive advantage to

Scottish business, which we would all welcome.'[7] Indeed. This is exactly what I and many others had been telling the Executive but they had steadfastly denied it, costing businesses nearly a billion pounds of identified costs plus unquantifiable costs of lost contracts, investment and jobs. I suppose I should be grateful for small victories.

As I was no longer a Conservative I was particularly interested to hear what the Tory member of the committee might say – after all, as the former Tory finance spokesman I had both publicly and privately taken every opportunity to push that group's policy towards a significant business rate cut rather than just parity. My greatest obstacle in this respect was David McLetchie, who, as leader, had given himself a policy veto and was not willing to go beyond restoring UBR (I suspected for fear of allowing in a Trojan horse that would encourage fiscal autonomy). With the irony that is the stuff of life, it was David who, as a backbencher, was now the Tory on the committee. Having established in the technical evidence session that preceded the debate that the Executive could still bring another order to Parliament to establish a new lower rate if its own motion was defeated, thus avoiding the problem of losing its income of £1.9 billion and being accused of being reckless (that didn't stop the minister doing so, of course), David supported my annulment. He ridiculed George Lyon for suggesting that a tax cut a year earlier than proposed would cause upset to businesses that had based their plans on Lyon's higher poundage. 'I cannot imagine', he said, 'that they will shed many tears if they get a revised bill telling them that their costs for running their business in 2006–07 will be less than they thought that they would be. That is the sort of news that is welcome to businesses rather than being a source of anguish or a cause of complaints about having to tear up plans and start again.'

He went on:

Mr Lyon and Mr McCabe are working on plans that will deliver something in the order of £745 million to £900 million-worth of cash-releasing savings in 2007–08. I think that it is remarkable that we can, apparently, conjure up such savings in the next financial year but cannot produce £70 million or £90 million in this financial year in order to achieve parity now. It strikes me as incredible that not a penny can be saved for this purpose in 2005–06 but, all of a sudden in 2007–08, £745 million can be released like a financial cascade of bounty.[8]

Although there were no rationally substantive arguments put by anyone against my proposal it made no difference and my annulment lost, with only David McLetchie supporting it (not being a member of the committee I could not vote for my own proposal). Again the nationalist on the committee, this time Bruce Crawford MSP, voted against, despite a supposed official policy supporting lower business rates.[9]

The poundage

Year	Scotland	England	Difference	(Wales)
2000/01	45.8	41.6	4.2	41.2
2001/02	47.0	43.0	4.0	42.6
2002/03	47.8	43.7	4.1	43.3
2003/04	47.8	44.4	3.4	44.0
2004/05	48.8	45.6	3.2	45.2
2005/06	46.1	42.2	3.9	42.1
2006/07	44.9	43.3	1.6	43.2
2007/08	44.4*	44.4*	nil	

The revenue

Year	Predicted	Collected	Income surplus	Poundage surplus
2000/01	£1540m	£1580m	£40m	1.2p
2001/02	£1554m	£1670m	£120m	3.4p
2002/03	£1570m	£1710m	£140m	4.0p
2003/04	£1590m	£1706m	£116m	3.5p
2004/05	£1873m	£1813m	-£60m	-1.6p
2005/06	£1931m	£1933m	£2m	nil

[*Estimated]

[Source: Scottish Local Government Financial Statistics, Scottish Executive Annual Expenditure Report 2003–04, p. 206, Scottish Executive Comparative Study of Business Tax Revenue. Scottish Executive non-domestic rates revaluation 2006/07, Valuation Office Agency (England & Wales).]

The Scottish Executive's own figures show that a business rates cut could have been afforded in the past and certainly could be delivered in the future. Between 2000 and 2006 the poundage differential varied between 4.2p and 3.2p, but the revealing aspect is how in five out of six years there was a surplus against the estimates of the amount collected. So, not only did the difference in poundage cost Scottish business £838 million against what they should have expected to pay, a further £358 million accrued to the Executive that could have been returned by discounting the following year's rate.

Most businesses do not pay corporation tax, but practically all pay non-domestic rates. To date Conservative policy has been to cut business rates to at least the level of that levied in England while the SNP policy has been to offer a cut without specifying at what level. Jack McConnell, bizarrely supported by the CBI Scotland, has effectively trumped these policies and will kill the debate unless any party is now brave enough to challenge the whole concept of a tax that hurts businesses whether they are profitable or not. As far as I am aware only Professor Sir Donald Mackay and myself have openly suggested the abolitionist solution. A review of three decades of international evidence by Young Lee and Richard H. Gordon suggests a reduction in business taxes of 10% can result in an increase in economic growth rate of between 1% and 2%.[10] Abolition could be achieved by reducing the poundage by 5.7p in the pound every year over eight years until it had gone altogether. If it's worth cutting the marginal tax rate why not continue until it is removed altogether, especially given the serious tax competition that Scotland faces from the Baltic and central Europe? Professors Donald Mackay and David Bell made a similar argument in their paper for the Policy Institute, *The Political Economy of Devolution*,[11] saying:

it would be perfectly possible, legally and politically, for the Scottish Executive to implement a policy of reducing business rates to zero over a four year period, and then maintaining a zero rate for, say, a further six years. Such a change would benefit new and small businesses particularly, as property costs are a fixed and high proportion of total operating costs for these types of businesses. It would also be beneficial in attracting new HQ functions to Scotland for, here again, property costs are an important consideration in location decisions.

The business rates currently takes £1.9 billion out of the Scottish economy from tens of thousands of businesses of all sorts (including not for profit operations) and into the hands of government, where it is distributed amongst thirty-two local authorities for them to spend on their priorities. The general consensus that the councillors and their officials are in a better position to make decisions about what this money should be spent on and that it will be beneficial to the taxed organisations paying it must be more forcefully challenged by the individual taxpayers themselves as well as their spokesmen and politicians.

Taking a look at the Scottish Assessors Association website is both revelatory and instructive as it illustrates what rateable values attach to different properties, say, in Edinburgh and elsewhere, and how reliefs can give some organisations significant advantages.

Typical rates bills in Edinburgh and elsewhere

Property	Rateable value	Rates relief	Rates bill
Traverse Theatre	£75,000	80%	£6,795
Royal Lyceum Theatre	£124,200	80%	£11,153
Festival Theatre	£183,000	80%	£17,092
Playhouse Theatre	£200,000	None	£85,870
The Filmhouse	£116,300	80%	£10,536
Revolution Night Club	£161,250	None	£72,562
Odeon Cinema	£165,000	None	£74,745
The Caledonian Hotel	£1,228,000	None	£556,284
The Balmoral Hotel	£1,240,000	None	£556,760
Jenners	£1,536,000	None	£689,664
Bank of Scotland, Head Office	£325,000	None	£146,149
The Scotsman	£1,630,000	None	£662,184
Scottish Widows, Head Office	£4,375,000	None	£1,981,875
Standard Life, Head Office	£4,760,000	None	£2,156,280

RBS, Head Office, Gogar	£6,550,000	None	£2,967,150
Edinburgh Airport	£6,860,000	None	£2,800,227
Edinburgh Royal Infirmary	£4,675,000	None	£2,117,775
HMP Edinburgh, Saughton	£1,220,000	None	£459,699
National Galleries	£383,500	80%	£34,438
National Portrait Gallery	£138,000	80%	£12,392
National Gallery of Modern Art	£80,595	80%	£13,721
Dean Gallery	£111,750	80%	£9,646
Almondvale Stadium, Livingston FC	£112,800	None	£48,210
Easter Road Stadium, Hibernian FC	£205,400	None	£93,046
Tynecastle Park, Heart of Midlothian FC	£234,000	None	£106,002
Murrayfield Stadium, SRU	£2,000,000	None	£832,616
Musselburgh Race Course	£60,000	None	£12,903
Karting Indoors, Tranent	£89,000	None	£40,317
Knockhill Race Track, Dunfermline	£15,500	None	£6,960
Abercorn Tennis Club	£13,500	None	£6,062
Alien Rock	£13,800	None	£5,668

[Source: www.saa.gov.uk. It should be noted that due to transitional relief, small business relief and small business supplement, properties of similar valuations can have quite different liabilities]

Publicly subsidised theatres, for instance, attract 80% relief as charities, while the private sector Playhouse pays more than the Traverse, Kings, Festival and Royal Lyceum theatres put together. After its relief the Filmhouse on Lothian Road pays less than £11,000, compared to the former Caley Cinema, which is now the Revolution nightclub, down the road and the Odeon up the road, both of which are liable for over £70,000. Galleries benefit from 80% relief but sports organisations do not, unless they are charitable. I do not argue that the 80% relief for charities, many of whom operate as businesses competing in the market, should be removed. I simply ask the question that if these organisations, which are far more commercial than they are often given credit for, find it hard to operate without such a discount then how difficult is it for those companies without the benefit of relief? Surely the relief should be extended to all?

The business rates bills for Jenners and the Princes Street book-ends of the Caley and Balmoral hotels are all above half a million pounds while Standard Life and the Royal Bank of Scotland head offices are both above £2 million and Scottish Widows is only a blink away. It should be remembered that these organisations all have further large offices in Edinburgh with rateable values above £1 million – and that's before considering the liabilities of the branch networks of the banks.

The use of a building rather than open space attracts greater liability, so the vast Knockhill race track has a smaller liability of £6,960 than the Karting Indoors warehouse shed at Tranent, which must find a whopping £40,317. This also compares with the small Abercorn tennis and squash club, which has a liability of £6,062 and the converted church that is Alien Rock climbing centre, set at £5,668. Clearly the rates bill will be a significant item of expenditure for many of these organisations, and while it may be dwarfed by the turnover of some it must be remembered it is a cost on the bottom line that has to be met irrespective of whether any profit is made. As soon as you open your doors you incur the liability.

Challenges

Critics of the reduction or removal of business rates argue that it would be cancelled out by rent rises, be unjust, unnecessary, unaffordable, or make financial stability unobtainable. I will take these in turn.

Rent rises

It is argued that a reduction in, or removal of business rates will result in the market compensating by raising the rents of properties and so there is little point in doing this. There are four reasons why this argument should be ignored. There is certainly some evidence that business rates are such a burden that they depress rental values and that some rental receipts have increased in areas where business rates have been removed (such as manufacturing facilities in Northern Ireland, DTZ report 2002). So what? The suggestion that owners of properties being able to increase their rents is a bad thing and that it would be better handing over company money to the state can only come from people who believe that the state knows best what to do with the money of individuals or their businesses. I come from the position that even if rentals rise then at least it stems from a contract willingly entered into rather than a confiscatory charge enforced with the power of law – in other words companies can threaten to move to properties with lower rents. Secondly, not all companies are the same; some actually own their properties (the Royal Bank, Scottish Widows, Edinburgh Airport and Standard Life being examples) and will only have the issue of rising rents to contend with where they have lease agreements. Thirdly, rentals are agreed over set periods and any opportunity to raise rents would not be immediate but would be a slow process, so many businesses would certainly benefit and when the rental review came might be able to break their lease if the increase was onerous. Finally, there is such a thing as the market and pressures on rentals can go up and down depending on the particular circumstances of the property at any given time. So yes, some rentals may go up, but they are unlikely to affect every business, are unlikely to be as much as the rates they are displacing and have the benefit of transferring funds within the private sector, rewarding investment decisions, leading to healthier profits for property developers and attracting further investment to improving property and, of course, resulting in a more healthy dynamic economy that pays more tax in other ways.

In response to calls for reductions in business rates the Scottish Executive has put forward a number of arguments that they have later made a complete U-turn on and others that are just spurious. I mention three.

Unjust?
The argument that the lower property values in Scotland required a justifiably higher poundage to deliver a similar yield was a nonsense as the whole point of having the same poundage was so that differing property values would make poorer areas across the whole of the UK more attractive to locate to or give existing firms some competitive edge. The immediate effect of increasing business rate poundage in Scotland was to make the properties in the poorer areas of the north of England especially advantageous. If this policy had been allowed to persist it could have been expected to begin to hurt Scottish companies trading accounts or the location of companies that had the flexibility to decide where they operate.

Unnecessary?

Another argument put by ministers was that total business tax revenues as a percentage of gross domestic product showed that only the USA and Ireland have a competitive advantage. Firstly, the business rate is not a tax: it is a standing charge that does not reflect profitability and penalizes businesses that require large or expensive properties over those that do not. Secondly, this approach shows a poverty of ambition – we should be looking to at least match if not beat the aggregate position of Ireland and give Scottish business the competitive advantage – why should we accept that Ireland and the USA should have it?

Unaffordable?

It is also claimed that if business rates were abolished then the loss of £1.9 billion would result in the closure of hospitals and schools. I answer elsewhere how savings can be found without wreaking havoc across Scotland's public services and there is also the likelihood of tax gains made elsewhere in Scotland from the improved business climate. Those points aside, however, it is also worth pointing out that the savings required to be found are significantly less than the Scottish Executive would have us believe. The reason for this is that the non-domestic rates are also levied on all government and public sector organisations. The Scottish Parliament alone pays a rates bill of £3.3 million to Edinburgh City Council from money given to it by the taxpayer. The Scottish Executive pays Scottish local authorities a total of £4.36 million[12] while there are over 150 non-departmental public bodies that receive funding from the Scottish Executive that then have to pay their rates – figures do not exist and are not collated but it will be a not inconsiderable sum. In addition there are all sorts of grant-aided private bodies that then pay their rates. The core grant support of public money often takes into account the business rate liabilities that organisations such as theatres, galleries and sports bodies have to pay. Again this is not available but will be in the millions.

Finally, all the local authorities have to pay business rates for their schools, administrative buildings, police stations, cleansing departments, etc. and from the research I have been able to compile

Business rate payments by the local authorities to themselves

Council	Total non domestic rates charged	Net rates charged to councils after reliefs	% of total charged to councils
Aberdeen	127,291,272	7,320,866	5.7
Angus	28,413,410	3,252,927	11.4
Argyll and Bute	27,239,706	2,712,263	9.9
Clackmannanshire	11,943,295	1,693,2992	14.2
Dundee	56,296,000	5,866,000	10.4
Dumfries & Galloway	35,477,315	4,400,973	12.4
East Ayrshire	27,054,178	3,655,321	13.5
East Lothian	15,090,985	2,250,572	14.9
East Dunbartonshrie	23,537,256	3,448,024	14.6
East Renfrewshire	11,486,000	2,847,594	24.8
Edinburgh	284,540,823	13,616,659	4.8
Eilean Siar	5,701,766	1,087,056	19.0
Falkirk	57,824,651	4,811,097	8.3
Glasgow	300,801,000	3,137,722	9.4
Highland	80,426,000	8,438,185	10.5
Inverclyde	20,073,000	2,751,000	13.7
Midlothian	19,445,000	2,957,278	15.2
North Ayrshire	33,183,796	4,237,608	12.8
North Lanarkshire	158,379,000	12,094,635	7.6
Orkney	6,953,000	1,345,456	19.4
Renfrewshire	71,788,618	4,999,157	6.9
Shetland	12,006,047	1,662,150	14.0
Stirling	40,347,803	3,177,846	7.8
South Ayrshire	34,814,182	3,848,589	11.0
South Lanarkshire	182,800,000	11,900,000	6.5
West Dunbartonshire	62,899,228	2,972,516	4.7
West Lothian	60,424,000	5,521,587	9.1
			Average
Totals:			11.5

Note: From a survey of all 32 Scottish local authorities requesting the non-domestic rates charged to their own departments 27 responded including Aberdeen, Glasgow, Highland and South Lanarkshire, revealing that there is an average of 11.5% of rates income that is Councils charging themselves for business rates. That suggests the abolition of rates would cost £222 million less at £1.71 billion, a saving of 5.3p on the poundage before we have started – almost equivalent to the £241 million or 5.7p poundage cut that I propose for reduction in the first year.

[Source: Survey of local authorities, Gingie Maynard / Brian Monteith 2006]

it runs at about 11.5% of council overheads. If this figure were to hold over all 32 councils it would suggest that local councils alone have to find £220 million to pay themselves and that this money comes either from the Scottish grant settlement, Council Tax or a mixture of both. In short, there is a great deal of money circulating in the system that would not require a saving to be stripped out. Not only is there an administrative futility saving to be made but it makes reducing business rates that much easier.

A cause of instablility?

I mentioned in the introduction the incredible position of CBI Scotland arguing that business rates should not be reduced below the uniform business rate (UBR) – and announcing in December that it has achieved a stability pact whereby none of the four major parties will cut the rate below that of England's. Let me explain why it is nothing more than a pantomime and a poor one at that.

Given that the business rate for England is set at Westminster in relation to the September RPI inflation figure, such a policy would mean that the Scottish Parliament would be foregoing the ability to set one of only two existing taxes that it can control – the business rate and the standard rate of income tax – and that it would be willing to ignore what economic conditions are saying for businesses in Scotland at any particular time. Such a policy, to all intents and purposes, would hand over the Scottish business rate to English MPs in perpetuity. The arguments for this truly bizarre position advanced by CBI Scotland Director, Iain McMillan, is that what businesses need above all else is stability and that if such a policy was to mean that the Scottish Executive was to receive more income than it might otherwise require in taxes, then it should return it to the benefit of the economy by investing it in infrastructure instead of returning it to the businesses through a tax cut or rebate. A more wrong-headed and anti-business position could not be expected from red-blooded revolutionary Tommy Sheridan.

Taking these points in reverse order, why the Director of CBI Scotland or its council should have any faith in any government expenditure to be efficient in delivering improved infrastructure and that any pro-rata increase in such spending will, in any event, provide demonstrable benefit is beyond belief. How would Iain McMillan know that expenditure on infrastructure was at any particular time not set to rise as a proportion of government spending anyway? Does the Director of CBI Scotland not believe that businesses will make better decisions for themselves if they are able to keep their money and invest it as they see fit? Does he not comprehend the advantages to Scottish businesses if the regressive and indiscriminate business rate poundage is cut and then businesses are charged for using infrastructure such as roads and bridges – helping both the public and private sectors to operate more efficiently and allowing the private sector not just to build but to finance and operate the infrastructure? But no, by implication, CBI Scotland would rather the public sector share of the economy stay as dominant and in fact grow (as it would under this policy).

The stability argument is simply laughable. It is suggested that if one Scottish Executive can cut the business rate then another could raise it – and that what Scottish businesses want to know is that they won't be paying any more than English companies pay. This is an argument that might have made sense in the 1997 referendum before the Scottish Parliament had been given the chance to set a business rate poundage – but after Jack McConnell took the opportunity to increase the business rates in 2000 that Rubicon had been crossed. Now two parties, the Scottish Liberal Democrats and the Scottish Nationalists, both advocate cutting rates below the UBR and the Scottish Conservatives have committed themselves to cutting the poundage to at least the UBR and might *contemplate* it going lower (how's that for vote-winning bravado?). The Labour Party is now isolated after being dragged embarrassingly by the skilful tactics of Nicol Stephen to a tax cutting position not of its choosing; otherwise it would appear less business friendly than its coalition partner. The momentum, suddenly, was with the tax cutters, until Iain McMillan stepped forward to 'announce' what might be called a 'stability pact' between parties that had not asked for and had not agreed to any such thing. The idea that any political parties other than the tax-obese Labour Party would sanction such a gentleman's agreement before an election and then keep to it after the elections is as risible as it is naïve. To achieve a position of stability, or more accurately, predictability, only requires that a government or potential government makes its intentions clear and has a credibility that it will stick to its policies. Thus, an announcement that the non-domestic rate poundage will fall by 4p in the pound every year or will increase by 2p every year is as stable as saying that it will not be any different from the poundage set by Westminster, tied to an inflation rate that cannot be predicted with certainty. The stability is in the route of direction, not in the rate, because the rate changes every year anyway.

The English poundage also has to take account of the revaluations of English properties so that the yield remains constant. So, by pegging the Scottish poundage to the rate set at Westminster the rate over time will have no stability or predictability in relation to the moving Scottish property values that Scottish businesses are aware of. Simply pegging the Scottish poundage to the English poundage delivers neither stability nor predictability; it is a chimera and a highly damaging one. It also displays an ignorance of what economic stability is – a school advocated by Gordon Brown, David Cameron and George Osborne, who argue that tax cuts and economic stability are incompatible. There is a great deal of evidence[13] such as Britain's own experience of pegging the pound to the Deutschmark and joining the Exchange Rate Mechanism, that it is monetary policy that is the most important determinant of economic stability rather than tax policy.

This of course has nothing to do with economics and everything to do with politics inside the British-orientated CBI, which cannot afford to be seen to be arguing for a situation where some of its members (in Scotland) are given a competitive advantage over others (in the rest of the UK).

Rates relief

In 2002, after a great deal of pressure from business organisations, most notably the Federation of Small Businesses and the Forum of Private Business, Scotland, the Scottish Executive introduced a small business rates relief. What it meant was that from April 2005 on a non-domestic property with a rateable value of £11,500 or less the owner would be eligible for a discount of between 5% and 50% on the rate poundage. This was not, however, a tax cut, for the scheme is substantially self-financing, with the owners of properties above £25,000 paying a supplement on the rate poundage. In 2003/04 when it was introduced the supplement was 0.6p on a rate poundage of 47.8p. This system represents a transfer of wealth from owners of the largest properties to the owners of the smallest properties. The amount this supplement can add should not be dismissed lightly: for instance, using the Scottish Executive's rates calculator in 2006/07, the Scottish Parliament could expect to pay an extra £30,480 in rates for the Holyrood Campus and Standard Life £19,040 for its head office in Lothian Road. The small business relief has to be claimed but the supplement is levied automatically, leading to the Scottish Executive making a profit in its first year of operation as the number of claims were fewer than budgeted for.[14]

The Scottish National Party intends to go a step further by proposing to give about 120,000 businesses with properties of rateable value of £8,000 or less a 100% relief, the further 30,000 business with properties between £8,001 and £10,000 a 50% relief, with those between £10,001 and £15,000 receiving a 25% relief. The Scottish Conservatives are believed to have adopted a similar scheme for their manifesto. Both claim they will deliver a uniform business rate, with only the Liberal Democrats suggesting they will actually cut rates to a level below the UBR.[15]

Benefits

By cutting business rates drastically Holyrood would demonstrate to the Scottish business community that it took its concerns seriously, wanted to help it and was prepared to act. Given the poor reputation that the Scottish Parliament has in business circles, such a policy would send a message of jaw-dropping proportions to the boardrooms of Scottish commerce. Secondly, it would show that the Scottish Parliament could use its tax powers to cut taxes and not just raise them, that it has matured and that it could, therefore, be trusted by the business community to have control over other taxes. Finally, it would of course give a much needed boost to the Scottish economy. A significant amount of fixed costs would be removed from businesses, who would be able to use those funds to reinvest in people or technology. Profitability would be improved and especially for the manufacturing sector some respite would be gained against the foreign competition that has lower costs generally.

So long as the Scottish Parliament shows no willingness to use the economic powers it already has at its disposal the argument about whether it should have greater responsibility will remain of interest only to politicians and their groupies. Furthermore, until a justifiably sceptical business community sees evidence of political parties offering genuine tax cuts any support for further financial powers will be tempered by a perception that fiscal autonomy means higher taxes. That advocates of fiscal autonomy continue to choose to talk about using taxes they don't have control over and to ignore the ones that they do is one of the more baffling aspects of the first eight years of devolution – unless they intentionally would rather destabilise the devolution settlement than help Scottish business?

Corporation taxes

It is often argued that the most important business tax that can be cut to invigorate the Scottish economy is corporation tax. As a fully signed up tax cutter I have no desire to rubbish any moves that will reduce taxes on business but I do feel that there are a number of points that need to be tackled in order for there to be lower corporation taxes in Scotland. These include questions of possibility, suitability and consequences.

Possibility?
The first point is that the power is not yet available. Delivering a low tax economy is as much about low politics as it is about high economics, if not more so. To obtain the power to reduce corporation tax (I hear no one saying it should be raised) far, far more has to be done to bring on-side the Scottish business community and the one thing that business people understand is

deeds. For outside observers, what politicians *do* is far more important than what they *say*. In commerce talk is cheap but the real achievement of growing a business and making profits consistently means sweating blood and dealing with often uncomfortable realities. So when business people hear politicians say they want to cut corporation taxes but don't have the powers in Holyrood they can be forgiven for being sceptical that tax cuts will ever happen. The SNP answer is that independence will deliver the powers, but the businessmen and women can't but notice that it could equally be achieved within the Union by a change in government policy – or a change of government itself. Corporation taxes could, for instance, be reduced across the whole of Britain (and should be in the face of mounting international competition). What then does the SNP do to bring about lower corporation taxes; does it argue vociferously at Westminster or seek to amend the Scotland Act so that the devolved parliament could have those powers? No, it is content to talk the talk in boardrooms up and down and in the parliamentary chamber but to say it is independence or nothing. In such circumstances talk is indeed cheap. Then when one looks at the SNP behaviour in regard to voting, which as an expression of intent is as good a measurement of deeds as one can expect in parliament, we consistently find that on issues from planning development, reduction of water charges, reliability of energy supply, public holidays, infrastructure investment and the reduction of business rates the SNP votes against what are generally understood to be in the interests of business. Scratch the surface and it is not difficult to find SNP speeches railing against profits, attacking open competition, defending protectionism, supporting subsidies and arguing for more and more regulation. I describe all of this not for some easy point-scoring partisan exercise – I have no need of it for I am not seeking election and am currently without a party – but because it is a tragedy in Scotland that the main opposition party displays a poorer understanding of business realities than the Executive parties. And yet an SNP that channelled its undoubted patriotism into arguing for a low tax, low regulation *and* small government approach would, I believe, pose a greater threat to the Union, just as I believe, paradoxically, that a Conservative Party that coupled the same economics with a greater emphasis on Scottish patriotism would be in a stronger position to defend the Union.

Even were a Scottish Executive to be formed by the SNP it would not have the power to adjust corporation tax. Even offering rebates would be problematic because identifying what are Scottish profits is all guesswork – as the SNP's own criticisms of the GERS report testifies. So I come back to the issue of business rates again. Not until the SNP shows in opposition – by voting regularly for a significant cut in Scottish business rates by, say, at least 12.5% – and delivering such a policy when in power – will it be in a position to bring businesses on board so that they are comfortable with either fiscal autonomy or full-scale independence.

Suitability?

The next point is that corporation tax is best suited to covering a single tax jurisdiction rather than varying within it. My point here is how does one decide where the profits of a company should be taxed? Scottish and Newcastle is an international company with its headquarters in Scotland. Although much of its profits will be earned overseas and although the majority of its domestic production is now in England there is no doubt that it is domiciled in Edinburgh. Were there to be a Scottish rate of corporation tax within the British union there would be little doubt that S & N would be liable for the Scottish rate. If the rate were low enough, a number of companies, possibly other brewers, would locate their head office in Scotland so that they could pay the lower corporation tax – but what constitutes a head office? Is it enough to be legally registered in Scotland? Is a brass plaque on a Charlotte Square door enough? Does the annual general meeting of the shareholders have to be held in Scotland, or *all* board meetings? These might appear to be minor points of detail but to me they go to the heart of the corporation tax argument because businesses and their markets do not always recognise borders – especially when within the UK there are none. The reason these and other questions need answers – and would undoubtedly require legislation, possibly at both Westminster and Holyrood – is that if it is easy to locate company profits in Scotland then it will also be easy to take them away again. Screwing and unscrewing a brass plate will simply screw up the economy.

So defining what is a Scottish company, liable to have its profits taxed in Scotland, is an important requirement for making any progress on vesting the power to vary corporation tax power at Holyrood and it is interesting that little attention has been given to this important problem. I can't help thinking that these issues are why cutting corporation tax is the favourite recipe for economic success talked (and talked) about by the SNP – because it would be cleaner and easier to deliver in a new jurisdiction of an independent Scotland than from within a borderless union that is the United Kingdom. Methinks the SNP would not be too keen to allow the Orkney and Shetland isles, for instance, to have their own corporation tax rate within an independent Scotland! The issue of definition is not insurmountable but it does need to be discussed so we can gauge to what extent it will allow the drive towards more location of businesses in Scotland, with the consequent increased investment to be realised – or if all that will move is the brass plates with little consequent benefit, except to corporate lawyers.

Reducing corporation tax can have beneficial effects to the economy from its effect on indigenous business as the attractions for investment become much improved. The tax's gradual reduction is, therefore, likely to proceed under governments of any hue at Westminster simply due to the pressures of tax competition.

Consequences?

This brings me to my third point, which is that just as a fiscally autonomous Scotland within the Union, or an independent Scotland, can reduce taxes to give itself a competitive advantage, so too can England. Would locating a business in Scotland be worth the candle if the corporation tax was cut to 15% but then England (or the rest of the UK) cut its rate to 16% – or lower? Again, I never hear advocates of lower taxes from within the SNP acknowledge that England is for so many of our businesses their main market, and for new businesses their first target market. If the UK or England were to be left to its own devices it would want to maximise the opportunities for its commercial sector by being more dynamic than Germany, Italy and France – the big economies of Europe – and what better way than to start taking its corporation taxes down. The threat from an economically aggressive England is, I believe, far more dangerous if Scotland were to become fully independent because it would mean that England would lose a deadweight of about forty Labour MPs at Westminster. This would significantly change the political balance and the prospects for patriotic tub-thumping tax-cutting Tory governments would be greatly enhanced.

There is also the possibility that a new Conservative government comes to power in London and makes little change to personal taxes but radically restructures the business tax regime. Such an approach would not sit uncomfortably with the George Osborne and David Cameron style of Conservatism. One has to ask if, under those circumstances, the low Scottish corporation tax argument would hold so much attraction? It may be that in such a landscape the best approach would be for a fiscally autonomous Scotland to retain the ability to make changes to corporation tax but to elect to have the tax collected on a UK basis and assigned to Scotland on an agreed formula, keeping administration costs for enterprise and government to a minimum.

In short, I believe there is a great deal of debate still to be had about the merits of varying corporation tax in Scotland so long as it remains within the Union, and that the political economy could change dramatically and quickly leave proposals without a great deal of merit. By contrast, the smart money in England is for the power to set business rates being devolved back to local authorities with a kaleidoscope of differing poundages being the outcome (ironically, killing stone dead the notion of a uniform business rate). Given that local authorities would see this new source of finance as a vital part of their income, and given that cutting business rates does not bring immediate financial rewards to local authorities as they do not yet have other taxes that can capture increased output and consumption, they would have little interest in cutting non-domestic rates. This would leave Scotland in a strong position to use significantly lower business, rates as a lever to attract business, reduce costs of existing enterprises, and realise the rewards in higher economic activity that under fiscal autonomy would be financially beneficial.

Although open to persuasion I remain to be convinced by the adherents of cutting corporation taxes in a devolved Scotland and believe that until those politicians that advocate it can demonstrate how it would work in a practical manner I will continue to advocate using the powers that already exist rather than talking about something that can't yet be done. For those who believe that if only Scotland had full independence they could then cut corporation taxes I say to them that they should demonstrate that they are genuine tax cutters by using the tools at their disposal – or remain disbelieved.

NOTES

1. See, for example, Eric M. Engen and Jonathan S. Skinner: 'Taxation and Economic Growth', NBER Working Paper No. W5826, November 1996, available at SSRN: http://ssrn.com/abstract=225613; W. Leibfritz, J. Thornton and A. Bibbee: *Taxation and economic performance*, OECD Economics Department Working Papers, No. 176, Paris, 1997; S. Folster and M. Henrekson: 'Growth and the public sector: a critique of the critics', *European Journal of Political Economy* 15.2, 1999, pp. 337–58.

2.

Business 3-year survival rates (1999–2002)

N. Ireland	72.4%
Wales	68.0%
England	66.4%
Scotland	65.3%

[Source: DTI]

3. Chris Masters (Chairman): *Nurturing Wealth Creation: A Report by the Scottish Manufacturing Steering Group*, Edinburgh, 2003.
4. Parliamentary Question S2W-6386 by Brian Monteith, answered 8 March 2004 by Jim Wallace.
5. Ernst & Young, *Scotland on Sunday*, 14 March 2004.
6. Official Report, Scottish Parliament Local Government and Transport Committee, 23 March 2004, Motion to annul the Non-Domestic Rate (Scotland) Order 2004: *For:* Brian Monteith (Con); *Against:* Bill Butler (Lab), Michael McMahon (Lab), Bristow Muldoon (Lab), Tommy Sheridan (SSP), Iain Smith (LD), Andrew Welsh (SNP).
7. Official Report, Scottish Parliament Local Government and Transport Committee, 18 April 2006, Col 3620.
8. Official Report, Scottish Parliament Local Government and Transport Committee, 18 April 2006, Col 3623.

9. Official Report, Scottish Parliament Local Government and Transport Committee, 18 April 2006, Motion to annul the Non-Domestic Rate (Scotland) Order 2006: *For:* David McLetchie (Conservative); *Against:* Andrew Arbuckle (Liberal Democrat), Bruce Crawford (SNP), Dr Sylvia Jackson (Labour), Paul Martin (Labour), Michael McMahon (Labour), Bristow Muldoon (Labour). Tommy Sheridan (SSP) opposed the motion but left before the vote.

10. Y. Lee and R.H. Gordon, 'Tax structure and economic growth', *Journal of Public Economics* 89, 2005, pp. 1027–43.

11. Sir Donald Mackay and David Bell: *The Political Economy of Devolution*, Policy Institute, Edinburgh, September 2006.

12. The amount paid by the Scottish Executive in non-domestic rates to local authorities does not include prisons or hospitals or other facilities of the NHS such as clinics. These are costs that will be stripped out reducing the total amount of savings that require to be found if business rates are cut year on year as I recommend. Source: Parliamentary Question S2W-27546 by Brian Monteith.

13. See the Reform website: www.reform.co.uk and search 'stability'.

14. SNP website: www.snp.org/campaigns/small-business/more-it-s-time-to-back-small-business.

15. Another distortion in the business rates system is how the 80% relief to charities is devastating our high streets. The reason for this is quite simple: charities are able to trade with an in-built advantage of an 80% relief on their rates and other tax advantages on VAT. Many of the charities are now retail multiples covering the whole of Britain with huge turnovers – competing against individual local shops. There's no need to remove the relief given to charities – all that is required is to extend it to all businesses by abolishing rates altogether.

Chapter 4

TRYING THE TARTAN TAX

'The current tax code is a daily mugging.'
– RONALD REAGAN

In previous chapters I've mentioned how Scotland's economy is underperforming. At a time when unemployment at 5.8% is 148,000[1] and we have the highest level of people in employment, such an accusation is still often dismissed; so let me put it another way. If Scotland's economy had grown at the same rate as England's since 1997 it would, by 2005, have been £5 billion larger.[2] That's a lot of wealth to raise standards of living or help employ the 100,000 people who have lost their manufacturing jobs over the same period.

You also can't argue with geography. For so many of our target markets we are further away than our competitors, enjoy poorer infrastructure and saddle our entrepreneurs with higher business taxes and far greater regulation. For instance, building the same new roadside travel lodge will cost 10% more here than it will in England, before the foundations are even laid, thanks to differences in building regulations that stipulate the requirement of an elevator to ensure disabled customers can reach the first floor, instead of simply being allocated ground floor rooms.

To address this self-imposed comparative economic disadvantage, to make Scotland a prosperous magnet for skilled workers, immigrants and entrepreneurs and to motivate those of us who just want to keep more of our hard earned pay, a cut in the standard rate of income tax by 3p would make a real difference.

The Scotland Act allows the standard rate, but not the lower (10p) or higher rate (40p), to be varied up or down by 3p. For every penny the standard rate is adjusted the income or loss is believed to be in the region of £290 million to the Treasury, so a threepenny variation would make a difference of plus or minus £870 million. There is a one-off administration cost that the Revenue and Customs would incur in establishing the procedures to administer and collect the different rate from Scottish taxpayers; this would have to be met by the Scottish Executive. During the 2003 Scottish elections Liberal Democrat leader Jim Wallace[3] conceded that the cost could be £200 million – a far cry from the £10 million estimate quoted in the Memorandum to the Scotland Bill (1997/98, Bill 104), but then the original white paper did suggest the new Scottish Parliament building would cost £40 million all in, including VAT.[4]

The effect of this set-up charge is that increasing the standard rate by only 1p brings only marginal benefit as two thirds of the expected income is consumed by the set-up cost. This creates an incentive to go for at least a 2p and probably a 3p increase to maximise the income benefit as quickly as possible. It should be recalled that the Treasury operates currently under its own rule, whereby if the tax rate is cut it will reduce the Scottish block grant by £290 million for every penny – in the belief that it will lose that revenue because of a lower tax rate. It therefore follows that if the standard rate is to be cut a saving of £290 million – £870 million – *plus the set up charge of £200 million* – will have to be found in the first year of the change.

Lower personal taxes are, for many, an incentive to work harder and produce more. Crucially, for the 251,000 self-employed in Scotland, who account for so much of our economic activity, lower personal taxes are more important than corporation tax. For all the debate about cutting corporation tax in Scotland it should be remembered that the self-employed – who pay a total tax of £1.4 billion – almost the same as the total Council Tax revenue in Scotland – do not pay any corporation tax at all.[5] The tax on their profits is their income tax, which, for all the write-offs and tax breaks that their accountants may find, very quickly moves from 22% to 40% on their taxable income. For anyone who is even modestly successful a Tartan Tax cut will be attractive, even though it can only deliver a maximum of a 3p benefit across the earnings to which the 22p standard rate applies.

Using the 2007–08 tax rates and allowances, the potential saving from a 3p cut in Tartan Tax would be nearly £1,000 per person. The calculation is the maximum net earnings possible after single person's allowance but before the top rate of tax kicks in – £33,300 – less the first £2,150 that is liable for the 10% rate – multiplied by £0.03. Using the formula below anyone earning less than £38,525 simply has to put their own gross earnings in, assuming they are only able to claim the personal allowance of £5,225 and nothing else (salary to a maximum of £33,300 + £5,225 = £38,525).

(Gross earnings of up to £38,525 – (personal allowance + first 10% taxable earnings)) x 3p
(38,525 – (5,225 + 2,150)) x 3p
(38,525 – 7,375) x 3p
31,150 x 3p = **£934.50**

For the tax cut to maximise its power to motivate and incentivise it would have to apply to the top rate of 40p too, but this power was withheld in the Scotland Act, most probably because Donald Dewar and Henry McLeish thought that if the top rate could be *increased* to 43p rather than cut to 37p it was likely to frighten the horses in the devolution referendum. I can assure you, as the manager of the No No campaign, there was absolutely no-one suggesting in that period that the tax, and especially the top rate, might ever be cut!

For our public services with employees in, say, teaching and nursing, lower marginal tax rates can make the difference between key staff staying in Scotland or going to other countries where the pay is higher or the tax lower. For East European migrants arriving in Britain, having a lower tax rate in Scotland would make it more attractive for the same job than England or Wales.

Can a tax cut be achieved, financially or politically? Critics argue that it would mean unacceptable job and service losses, a reduction in the Scottish block grant and/or outright opposition from the Treasury. Some also maintain that a cut in income tax would be too complex to administer.

It is true that there are technical difficulties that need to be ironed out. Douglas Mayer, a former Scottish office civil servant in the finance department and regular contributor to the letters pages of *The Scotsman* and *The Herald*, has argued that the income tax attributable to Scotland may have to be adjusted further to take account of people living in Scotland whose tax base is in England and whose tax accrues in the English figures. Similarly, Scots living in England, with a Scottish taxation source, might also cause a complication to the calculation.

Such issues are not, however, beyond the wit of man and various rules already exist in determining liabilities and levels of income for people who work and live in certain jurisdictions within the union such as the Isle of Man, Jersey and Guernsey. Tax is a technical business and requires manuals and guidelines to apply it, but the idea that solutions could not be found or that it would require a complexity that is beyond us does not seem reasonable when one considers the work of Gordon Brown in tax regulation in the last ten years.

Solutions can also be found to the financial and political objections raised above.

People are employed and services are delivered using taxes, so surely a cut in taxes means swingeing cuts, so brutal that nobody will vote for them? There are two answers to this question, depending on what you believe happens when taxes are cut. If you believe, as the Treasury believes and the received wisdom holds in Scotland, that tax cuts mean a loss of revenue that must be funded by a comparable reduction in spending, then savings in public services will need to be found.

When one considers that in the last eight years Scotland's budget has grown by £10 billion, from about £15.6 billion to £25.8 billion, then it is surely possible to find savings of £870 million without the end of our public services as we know and love them. For instance, simply pegging public spending at present levels rather than letting it grow would itself provide significant savings. The efficiency gains factored in to the Scottish Executive's latest budget for 2006–07 are claimed to be in the region of £745 million[6] – a figure that is disputed – nevertheless, if that sum had been used to cut taxes, essentially returning the savings to the taxpayer rather than spending them on, arguably, more inefficient services, then a 3p cut in the standard rate could surely be delivered by a more prudent Scottish Executive.

Alternatively, if you believe, as Professor Arthur Laffer has argued, and the experience of many governments has shown, that a marginal drop in personal tax rates can act as an incentive to raise productivity, bringing higher personal and business earnings with consequent higher consumption, then higher tax receipts will be delivered. Thus, public service cuts are not necessarily required and a marginal tax cut can be at least self-financing, if not produce a surplus.

In such a scenario there will be a time lag between the cut in taxes that will produce an initial fall in receipts and the subsequent productivity gains that will produce a tax bounty. This is normally covered by temporary government borrowing, but as the Scottish Parliament has no powers to borrow it would either have to obtain those powers, generate additional funds through privatisations or reduce its spending, albeit for a temporary period – so long as the Treasury agreed to pass on the increased revenue when it arrived. This brings us to the next issue: establishing an agreement with the Treasury that the proceeds of any tax cut should come to a new Scottish Exchequer.

This is a political question, not an economic one, and it would be for the First Minister of the day to hold meetings with the Chancellor and possibly the Prime Minister to broker a deal whereby the proceeds of improved economic growth on the basis of any Scottish tax cuts would accrue to Scotland. The First Minister's case would require that before any tax cut there should be close monitoring of economic indicators so that the expected growth before any tax cuts could be agreed and the revenues from income tax in Scotland definitively identified. After the change is introduced any income above the anticipated level (remember the Treasury would expect it to be £270 million less for every penny cut) would then be passed on to Scotland. In this way the Treasury would be saving money on the Scottish block grant but would recompense the Scottish Executive for any above par economic improvement.

Savings, of course, do not necessarily come from shedding jobs, but are often achieved by simply doing things differently. For instance, our government could move Scottish Water into the private sector, just like all the water utilities in England and Wales. This would leave the utility to find as much investment capital as it required on the market; relieving the government of the £181 million[7] it invests every year.

There are, of course, two other political questions that demand answers. The first is the impact that a Scottish tax cut will have on the maintenance of the block grant and the accompanying Barnett Formula. This is consistently levelled by unionists and is one of the reasons why the Scottish Conservative leadership has not embraced a Tartan Tax cut (the others being a lack of spleen and a long-standing absence of what might normally pass for any economic philosophy of its own). The second question is: what if the Treasury refuses to budge and is not willing to see that additional tax revenues generated from a more dynamic economy brought about by decisions taken in Edinburgh rather than London are returned to the Scottish Executive?

Michael Forsyth has, on a number of occasions, most recently following the publication of his Tax Commission[8] report, stated that if a Scottish Executive were to cut the standard rate of tax in Scotland it would result in a political reaction amongst English MPs, probably across parties, that would bring about the end of the Barnett Formula. Why, they would ask, are we delivering more money for Scotland to spend on education, health and policing – and then letting them have lower taxes as well? It would be an abundantly fair question. Of course, with the Treasury rule about deducting the supposedly lost revenue that would result from a tax cut being activated, the question is answered in part, but, crucially, not completely. Forsyth is right, advocating a Tartan Tax cut must be accompanied by a willingness to acknowledge, if not actually advocate, that the current system of funding the Scottish Executive would have to change. Barnett would maybe not be dead in the water but it would certainly be drowning – and there would be little point in looking around for straws to clutch. English MPs would still notice that, even with a cut in Scottish spending to finance a tax cut, the per capita spend on devolved public services would still be greater than in England. The Barnett Formula would still be put into play and any Scottish politician advocating a Tartan Tax cut would have to recognise in advance that its continued existence would be highly unlikely. This does not trouble me: as I have already argued, there was a time when Barnett and the block grant were appropriate, but no longer do I believe that is the case. The system is injurious to Scotland's body politic and is sustaining a dependency culture that goes to the heart of our slovenly political thinking and our poorer economic performance.

That there is no such political dilemma for those politicians who might want to increase the Tartan Tax (Alex Salmond, John Swinney, Jim Wallace – is there anyone still willing to admit they advocated it?) has always been one of flaws in the financial arrangements. Nevertheless, there is no point in arguing for a Tartan Tax cut without being ready to promote the case for some form of fiscal autonomy – for they are like brother and sister to each other. Without the ability to vary, collect and have assigned a wider range of taxes, there is little doubt that Scottish revenue would be significantly reduced by any new formula and public services would face significant cuts. For those of us who believe fiscal autonomy is the way Scotland and its new Parliament should proceed there is little to fear politically other than fear itself. The Forsyth warnings, although sincere and rational, are political old think that we must now move on from.

The second difficulty – namely, what if the Treasury doesn't play ball – can now be seen as Scotch mist, for the Treasury would itself want to enter into negotiations to determine a new settlement, otherwise Scotland would be left with higher spending and lower taxes – a political outcome that MPs across England would find hard to stomach. Yes, it could even, while some intemperate MPs mouthed off and radio talk shows whipped up outrage about the Scots having their cake and eating it, look as if the Union itself might be placed in jeopardy, but once a new formula based on fiscal autonomy with a glide path to deliver it was agreed, then calmer voices would return, for it would be in the interests of everyone but Scottish and English nationalists to find a new dispensation.

Conservative critics cite another political difficulty. But the excuse given to the media that tax cuts can't be offered by Scottish Conservatives in any elections for fear of confusing the message of 'stability before tax cuts', thus upsetting David Cameron or Shadow Chancellor George Osborne, is so lame that no Zimmer frame could help it stand up to scrutiny. Osborne and David Cameron have both made it clear repeatedly that it is for Goldie and her group to make their own taxation proposals. All they want is to see the Tories begin to win and they are happy to let the party in Scotland do its own thing – even if that runs contrary to what they have been trying in England. The reality is that the Scottish Tories have simply not done the work to establish how the tax cuts can be afforded and little attention is given to the work of other academics who have identified savings and efficiency gains. Secondly, the current leadership is petrified that a Tartan Tax reduction would trigger a division in the party because it would open the door for fiscal autonomy. The leadership refuses to confront the issue and appears to be waiting to be forced to formulate a policy. What is more likely is that the leadership will be changed as a consequence.

To summarise, a significant income tax cut is possible, whether it is funded by efficiency gains or the generation of additional revenue; it is desirable, because it has the power to rejuvenate our economy; it is necessary if we are to challenge Scotland's complacent collectivist consensus to its roots; and it is right because it helps individuals and families make more appropriate choices for their lives than second-guessing politicians or officials ever can. It's a policy that's long overdue, but is anyone brave enough to attempt it?

NOTES

1. Scottish Economic Statistics, Scottish Executive, November 2006.
2. Scottish National Party: *The Cost of London Labour*, November 2006.
3. Jim Wallace, *The Scotsman*, 11 April 2003. In his statement to Parliament on 24 June 1999 (Official Report Col 811), Finance Minister Jack McConnell had said the cost of administration would be £20 million with a £2.5 million annual running cost.
4. The white paper issued for the devolution referendum estimated 'the costs to the government of establishing the mechanisms for tax variation at £10 million, with running costs at about £8 [*sic*] per annum'. It should be noted that white papers are not mere guesstimates but do require due diligence by the departments that draw them up.
5. Her Majesty's Revenue and Customs.
6. Scottish Executive Efficiency Savings Technical Note, September 2005.
7. Scottish Executive Draft Budget 2006–07.
8. Michael Forsyth (Chairman): *Tax Matters, Reforming the Tax System*, Report of the Tax Reform Commission, London, 2006.

Chapter 5

FLATTENING TAXES

*'The hardest thing in the world
to understand is the income tax.'*
– ALBERT EINSTEIN

In a quiet policy revolution, the likes of which has not been seen since the 1980s when Thatcher and Reagan were dominating the free democratic world, the idea of a one single rate of income tax – a flat tax – is gaining ground in the emerging nations of Europe, increasing tax competition with older, less dynamic countries and causing politicians of developed economies such as Germany and Britain to consider the policy. In his Adam Smith Institute paper[1] Richard Teather puts it succinctly: 'In the 1980s the UK led the way in tax reform; now the question is whether we can keep up or be left behind.'

A flat tax used to be an exotic concept used only in small places such as Hong Kong, Jersey and Guernsey. In the 1980s there was no larger country willing to try an experiment that could risk tax revenues plummeting, with a consequential public finance crisis. Then, thanks to Thatcher and Reagan, what seemed a miracle happened: communism imploded. New democratic governments were formed and pretty soon they found that, while their economies could, with western expertise, modernise quickly, their populations were not at all enamoured with paying western levels of personal taxes. Revenue collection was low and erratic and public finances were consequently unpredictable. This weakness provided an opportunity, for with nothing to lose and everything to gain some emerging East European democracies decided that a flat tax could be tried. Since that moment the debate about a flat tax has no longer been just about an attractive theory but also about what the evidence shows happens when countries adopt a flat tax.

The first nation to adopt the flat tax was Estonia in 1994; the change precipitated the stunning rise in economic fortunes of that country. Within ten years of the collapse of Soviet style socialism its situation completely changed. Estonia's economy is unrecognisable; mass absolute poverty has been successfully tackled and social welfare has improved along with it. Estonian spending power per head is five times that of a Cuban and four times that of a Serbian. It has already surpassed that of a Chilean or Uruguayan and is only half that of us Brits – but gaining fast. How was this achieved? One former Prime Minister of Estonia, Mart Laar, who held office twice, 1992–94 and 1999–2002, says there were three key lessons.[2] The first was to understand the crucial importance of the rule of law. The second was that governments must be decisive about reforms and stick with them, despite the short-term pain they often bring. The third, and most vital, was that change had to take place in the minds of the people:

> In the era of socialism, people were not used to thinking for themselves, taking the initiative or assuming risks. Many people had to be shaken free of the illusion – common in post-communist countries – that, somehow, somebody else was going to come along and solve their problems for them. It was necessary to energise people, to get them moving, to force them to make decisions and take responsibility for themselves.

This required the encouragement of competition through low regulation, exemplified by trade not aid, and low taxes, exemplified by a flat rate income tax of 26% – since cut even lower – and no taxation of business profits reinvested in domestic businesses.

Estonia's Baltic neighbours Lithuania and Latvia soon followed her example, and in the last couple of years great swathes of central and Eastern Europe have signed up to the revolution (see table below). None of these countries now want to turn the clock back, and indeed the only question is whether they should cut the tax rate even further.

Examples of flat taxes

Country	Year adopted	Rate %
Estonia	1994	24
Lithuania	1994	33
Latvia	1995	25
Russia	2001	13
Serbia	2003	10
Ukraine	2003	13
Slovakia	2003	19
Georgia	2005	12
Romania	2005	16

[Source: 2006 Index of Economic Freedom]

For practical proof of success in raising revenue, we need look no further than Alvin Rabushka's analysis of the Russian experience.[3] In Russia, a 13% flat tax was implemented on 1 January 2001. Income tax revenue for 2001 rose 25.2% in real terms; in 2002 it was up 24.6%, in 2003 a further 15.2%. There is no doubt that some of Russia's revenue growth has come by attracting people who once avoided paying tax, legally or illegally, to become taxpayers; but so too has it encouraged existing taxpayers to work harder and grow the economy. In Britain we too have many people, rich and poor, who seek to avoid tax by operating in the black economy or living abroad. These people would find it more attractive to pay British taxes, many for the first time in their lives.

Other countries actively considering introducing a flat tax system include Poland and the Czech Republic. Germany has toyed with the idea.[4] In the United States George Bush has advisers looking at the flat tax. In Spain, Prime Minister Zapatero, another leader of the left, is interested in the concept and has been joined by the leaders of Communist China. Flat tax is increasingly seen not as a right-wing concept, but as a progressive move that is, in many ways, above ideology.

But, as Allister Heath deduces correctly in his comprehensive review of flat taxes and their effects, *Flat Tax: Towards a British Model*,[5] campaigns for a flat tax – just like tax cuts – cannot be added on to election strategies at the last moment, but require a strategic campaign which shows the benefits to the poorest in society – this means emphasising the moral case.

What has made the idea so alluring, what is the theory and how could it be applied in Britain or a fiscally autonomous Scotland? A flat tax has many arguments in its favour: it is simple to understand and apply, it reduces tax avoidance and evasion, it can increase tax revenues, it incentivises work and – most surprising to the uninitiated – it can especially help the poorest and it is fair. Opponents counter that 'it's not fair; it's a sop to the rich', and that the country can't afford it.

Taxation in Britain is currently very unfair. Too many people on low incomes pay tax when they should be exempt, and too many hard-pressed moderately paid workers are dragged into top-rate tax. For example, some part-time workers earning the minimum wage pay tax, and some teachers pay top-rate tax. There are many ways to describe such a system, but fairness is surely not one of them. A flat tax for Britain would work on a basic principle – the low-paid pay nothing and everyone else pays the same rate on each earned pound. There are only two variables; the threshold below which no tax is paid, and the tax rate above that threshold. Because of the existence of the threshold – set two or three times higher than the current level – as someone earns more they actually pay a greater proportion of their overall income in tax than those earning less. Similarly, under a flat tax high earners actually end up paying a greater percentage of a country's tax take than they pay under our current graduated tax, because the incentive to evade or avoid tax evaporates, and the incentive both to earn more and to shift money from sheltered investments to productive and taxable investments increases. This is precisely what happened in Britain during the time when Conservatives cut the top rate from 83% to 40% – the top 10% of earners went from paying 35% of the total take in 1979 to 42% in 1990.

The flat tax recognises the key to a free and decent society, as it places a limit beneath which no person is allowed to fall, but places no limit on how high a person can rise. The marginal tax rate on the extra pound beyond, say, £14,000 is identical to the rate on the extra pound beyond £114,000 or £1,114,000. It would encourage people to make the best of themselves, safe in the knowledge that the state would not attempt to hold them back in the way that Old Labour's socialism or New Labour's managerialism does. People would seek opportunity and flourish rather than being levelled down in the name of 'equality' or 'inclusion'.

For the idea to work in practice, as well as being flat, the tax must be low in comparison to the current level of taxes. As has been argued earlier, taxation in Britain is far too high, and lower taxes have economic, social and moral benefits for which the case must be put. Lower tax is not about helping the rich; lower taxes allow people to decide how to spend their own money. They allow individual choice to be placed above government intervention, freedom to reign over coercion, and encourage the personal responsibility on which free societies are built. Lower taxes encourage a giving culture where self-help blossoms. In a low-tax country like the United States, charitable donations are three times higher, per household, than they are in high-tax Britain.[6] That's because when a government tells people it is taking more tax from them so it can help the vulnerable, people paying tax can feel they have discharged their duty.

This prompts the fundamental question of how do we pay for a flat tax? There are two answers to this question, both of which create the opportunity for a low, flat tax.

The first argument states that before we decide what we want to do we have to work out what we can afford. For those who would make such a decision based on 'household economics' there are various ways to finance the tax cut. Firstly, substantial amounts of money would be saved because it is much cheaper to administer a simple tax code than the current complicated one. For those who dismiss this as insignificant, consider that the cost of administering the federal income tax in the United States is greater than the entire federal budget deficit and that the 8 billion pages of forms that the IRS sends to 100 million American taxpayers is enough to stretch 28 times around the earth. Our system may be less complicated than theirs, but it is not small beer, as Allister Heath and others can demonstrate.

Moreover, spending reviews carried out by the Taxpayers' Alliance and also by David James in 2004 identified £81 billion and £35 billion respectively of Whitehall savings. One estimate concludes that the £81 billion would be enough to balance the Treasury books after a flat tax of 22% with a £20,000 personal allowance. Thirdly, there must come a point in Scotland where we look at the vast volumes of money being spent on unreformed public services and say 'enough is enough'. The theory of being able to improve our public services through money alone has been tested to destruction, and the track record of failure is glaring. Public services in Scotland are better funded than in most European countries, but European standards put Scotland to shame, exposing our services as often second rate. There is sufficient money being wasted on these behemoths that could be given back to the taxpayers who have worked hard for it, as explained in the previous chapter. So, for household economists the tests are met.

The second argument recognises that Britain, however, is not a household. As a country we should reject the household economics approach and rediscover Laffer economics, especially after seeing it work so spectacularly in the era of Thatcher and Reagan. Legend has it that in 1976 Art Laffer sketched the Laffer Curve on a napkin in a restaurant, showing that tax revenue is zero at tax rates of 0% (self-evidently) and 100% (because there is no incentive to work), and that there is some optimal rate of tax in between at which revenues are maximised, showing that tax cuts can increase tax revenue. Reagan's Kemp-Roth Tax Cut (so named after its Congressional sponsors) was followed by an increase in tax receipts. This is the argument we must articulate in Scotland. Here's the evidence from the Adam Smith Institute:[7] 'if you look at the bottom 50%, you'll find that they paid 8.3% less in tax in 1984 than they did in 1981. In contrast, the share for the top 5% of taxpayers increased; in 1981 they paid 35.3% of the total income tax collected; in 1984 they paid 38.9%.'

We don't need to find money for a flat tax: it can pay for itself so long as it is set at the right rate – a rate low enough to encourage greater productivity, to attract economic migrants and new investment and to see tax 'avoision'[8] reduced through the declaration of more earnings.

A look at Scotland's particular economic problems relative to the rest of the UK and at the march of the emerging East European states suggests Scotland cannot afford *not* to cut taxes.

Making the policy work

For the policy to work in Scotland, we would need to take the following steps:

1. Acknowledge that national insurance is simply income tax by another name and merge the two so that the true level of taxation is identified and fully understood by the public. Given that benefits and entitlements such as pensions are not paid out of what you have contributed but are funded from current revenues, it makes sense to be transparent and make our systems far simpler. Based upon current contributions this would add about 11p to the tax rates, changing current rates from 10p to 21p, 22p to 33p and 40p to 51p – although there would be some adjustments that would need to be taken into account as top rate taxpayers currently have a ceiling on contributions. With visible tax rates of 21p, 33p and 51p the realisation that British taxation is comparatively high in real terms and against international competitors would introduce further pressures for lowering the rates. (The employers' contributions could be managed by a rate linked to the income tax, possibly capped, if it was thought this tax on employment should be retained. Personally I would seek to phase it out, leaving just corporate taxes on consumption and profits.)

2. Following research and debate, set a threshold for the commencement of paying tax that would be linked to the average

wage, e.g. the first 45% being tax free, which at present would be around £12,000. The purpose would be to take the low paid out of tax liability altogether, thus removing the nonsense of taking tax from them with one hand and then having to give them income-related benefits with another. In 2001 Maurice Saatchi and Peter Warburton[9] pointed out the extent to which our tax and benefits system overlaps:

> Every year, the government collects around £30 billion in income tax and national insurance contributions from working households to whom it also distributes around £30 billion in benefits. So, bizarrely, Britain's tax and benefit system today needlessly transfers £30 billion each year (9% of all government spending) in and out of the very same working age households, because of the overlap between taxpayers and recipients of state-administered benefits and pensions.
>
> Meanwhile, the requirement to pay income tax has never reached so low down the income scale. 3.6 million people of working age earn less than half the national average. (£21,842 p.a. at April 2000). Virtually all of them pay tax to the government. And the majority of them also receive means-tested benefits from the government. Some of these benefits are themselves taxed. The result is that tens of millions of benefit claims have to be paid each week, many of which are income top-ups and housing subsidies to tax-paying low income working households.

3. Set a single flat rate of income tax in the region of the new standard rate of 33% (22% without national insurance), preferably lower. Richard Teather has calculated[10] the costs of having a flat tax at the current 22% rate (without merging national insurance) and having different personal allowances:

Cost of flat tax

*Tax loss from having a single flat tax rate of 22%, with an
increased personal allowance as shown*

| New Personal Allowance (£) | Reduced tax revenues | | Total £ billion |
	Increasing PA £ million	Abolishing top rate £ million	
7,500	11,735	18,107	29
10,000	26,285	16,592	42
15,000	49,970	13,561	63
20,000	65,795	12,182	78

[Source: Inland Revenue data, 2004/5]

If these economic losses of £29 billion, £42 billion, £63 billion and
£78 billion are taken as a given then it can be seen that even the
modest savings of £35 billion identified by the James Committee
could allow a new personal allowance of £7,500. If the Taxpayers'
Alliance savings of £81 billion are correct then a personal
allowance of £20,000 is a possibility. It should also be noted that
the cost of abolishing the top rate of tax is lower for new higher
levels of personal allowance, because increasing the personal
allowance takes people out of the higher rate band. Abolishing the
higher rate tax on its own would initially reduce tax revenues by
roughly £20 billion. Teather's preference is for a modest £12,000
allowance, which would remove one million taxpayers from the
current liability to pay income tax. His calculations are conservative, given that he has not allowed for any Laffer effect of
increased revenues from greater productivity and less tax avoision.
For comparison the following table shows the current tax rates and
those proposed by Saatchi and Warburton, and by Teather. There
are further models by Allister Heath and others.

British income tax rates and alternatives suggested

Current rates 2006–07		Saatchi & Warburton proposal		Teather proposal	
Salary band	tax rate	Salary band	tax rate	Salary band	tax rate
£0–£5,035	0%	£0–£9,999	0%	£0–£11,999	0%
£5,036–£7,125	10%	£10,000–	26%	£12,000–	22%
£7,126–37,435	22%				
£37,436–	40%				

[Source: HM Customs and Revenues for tax year 2006–07 based upon personal allowance only for single person under 65]

Further work by Teather shows in detail how the lowest paid benefit more than the highest income group, with the poorest third benefiting more than the richest third.

Who benefits?

Effect of current income tax system, compared with flat tax of 22% with £12,000 personal allowance

Families:	Average income (£)	Current UK tax (% income)	Flat tax (% income)	Saving (% income)
Poorest 10%	2,549	9.2	0	9.2
2nd	4,280	7.9	0	7.9
3rd	6,811	9.8	0	9.8
4th	11,464	12.1	0	12.1
5th	16,792	11.9	6.0	5.6
6th	21,696	12.8	9.8	3.0
7th	28,427	14.0	12.7	1.3
8th	35,571	14.9	14.6	0.3
9th	44,981	16.3	16.1	0.2
Richest 10%	79,187	20.1	18.7	1.4

[Source: Figures derived from Office of National Statistics]

These calculations are for personal taxes, but a flat tax should also result in companies' profits being taxed at the same rate. This has the benefit of removing the current scope for tax avoidance caused by the different tax treatments of individuals and companies, and ensures that all income is taxed once and once only.

The effect of the growth of tax on the poorest paid can be illustrated by using the Tax Freedom Day measurement.[11] The Adam Smith Institute has calculated that in 1997 the average taxpayer had to work until 26 May to pay for that year's taxes but by 2006 this had climbed to 3 June. Saatchi and Warburton say that for the poorest the tax freedom day is an astonishing 18 August. Introducing a flat tax using higher tax threshold would alter this injustice drastically.

In his work Heath has usefully summarised some thirty-six academic studies which illustrate the various benefits that have made the idea so attractive and have challenged the opponents of the idea in the UK Treasury to 'rebut every piece of contrary evidence'. He goes on to suggest his own model, with a tax-free allowance of £9,000; an income tax rate of 22% for those of pensionable age and a rate of 28% for those of working age (thus allowing for the merging of income tax and national insurance); no tax on investment income; capital gains tax and inheritance tax abolished. He's certainly my sort of tax cutter! Heath estimates that, using Treasury figures, the initial 'lost' income will be £60 billion but that, following a Gershon style review, pegging public spending growth to less than that of the economy's, improving revenue and some revenue-earning privatisations, that the difference can be reduced to only £9 billion. This could be covered by borrowing less than the amount Gordon Brown proposes under the current regime. What is clear from this and other work by Teather, Grecu, Saatchi, Warburton, Hall and Rabushka is that there is no lack of evidence or models upon which to base a British – or Scottish – system that could work.

A flat tax could be introduced in Scotland if it were fiscally autonomous – or independent – and the east European experience shows it would be ideally suited to a country of Scotland's size. If former Communist countries can use a flat tax to reinvigorate their dormant economies, so too could proto-Communist Scotland, with its large public sector and the dependency culture that goes with it. In a country that is still searching for a route back to the entrepreneurialism and inventiveness of its glorious past, a flat tax could provide a yellow brick road to success.

NOTES
1. Richard Teather: *A Flat Tax for the UK – a Practical Reality*, Adam Smith Institute, London, 2005.
2. Mart Laar: 'How Estonia did it', in *2003 Index of Economic Freedom*, The Heritage Foundation, Washington DC, 2003.
3. Alvin Rabushka: 'The Flat Tax at Work in Russia; Year Three', 2004, available at russianeconomy.org/comments/042604.html
4. Angela Merkel, the CDU leader, appointed Paul Kirchof, the most vocal advocate of a German flat tax, as her campaign finance spokesman in the 2005 elections and it became a hot topic of debate but its reception was mixed. Following the inconclusive election Kirchof went back to academia while Merkel sought Social Democratic support for her to become Chancellor, effectively killing the idea.
5. Allister Heath: *Flat Tax: Towards a British Model*, The Taxpayers' Alliance / Stockholm Network, London, 2006.
6. Karen Wright: 'Generosity versus Altruism', *Voluntas* 12.4, Baltimore, 2002.
7. James Gwartney: 'Tax Rates versus Tax Revenues', in *It pays to cut Taxes*, Adam Smith Institute, London, 1984.
8. The term 'Avoision' was coined by Arthur Seldon to describe the grey area between tax avoidance and tax evasion in *Tax Avoision*, Institute of Economic Affairs, London, 1979.
9. Maurice Saatchi and Peter Warburton: *Poor People! Stop paying tax!*, Centre for Policy Studies, London, 2001.
10. Teather: *A Flat Tax for the UK – a Practical Reality*.
11. For Tax Freedom Day information see www.adamsmith.org/tax/

Chapter 6

SELLING THE SALES TAX

'I am proud to be paying taxes in the United States.
The only thing is – I could be just as proud for half the money.'
— ARTHUR GODFREY

Like so much of Scotland's economic activity, our local authorities live in their own dependency culture, for they too are dependent on the munificence of central government. The answer to this problem is to completely restructure local government finance – not just the local taxation, which only manages to raise a paltry 16.7%[1] towards total council spending – but the responsibilities that lead to that spending too. Without asking, 'What is local government for?' and the accompanying, 'What, therefore, should local government do?' can we begin to see what global sums require to be raised, what, if any central government support should be provided and what is the best way to raise the remaining sum.

Talk of abolishing the Council Tax – if that is the best thing to do – can then be given serious consideration. To research and discuss the alternatives to Council Tax without looking at why any local taxation is required is futile and doomed to failure – as the recent publication of the Burt Committee's report showed back in November 2006.

With an average rise of 60% since 1997, Council Tax is undoubtedly the cause of great anxiety for many, especially those on fixed incomes such as pensioners, and is probably the most despised tax in Scotland. It should be recalled that Council Tax was, rather ironically, only introduced as a panic measure in John Major's haste to dump the similarly divisive poll tax. The reality is that if we were to construct a more equitable and accountable model of how we finance local government we would not be where we are now.

If the answer to the first question, 'What is local government for?' is that it is to deliver central government policy then it should be centrally designed, funded and directed, with little room for local variation other than what demography and topography requires. We might call this the Irish model, where local government is essentially the local administration of the Dublin government's policies, with the chief executives of councils appointed by the Minister for Local Government and councillors allowed only limited powers. Consequently, the funding is direct from Dublin with no domestic rates (abolished by Taoiseach Jack Lynch in 1977) and only a small number of charges for rubbish collection, schoolbooks and school meals to provide independent income.

If the answer is that we want local public services to reflect the needs and aspirations of distinct communities, large or small, then we need authorities that have the economic freedom to act, and are responsive to, their communities' interests. We might call this the American model, where elections are held for a wide variety of positions, local ordinances can be set by plebiscite and taxes vary widely to ensure they are not only empowered but free from central direction.

In Britain we have neither one model nor the other, but instead a complex *mille feuilleté* with thousands of layers of guidelines and highly complex funding calculations. This local government structure was never conceived and sold by political leaders to the British public, nor did it happily evolve through a process of trial and error. Rather it is the progeny of political expediency over the last forty or more years by governments of all colours and philosophies.

It appears to me that we have two choices: we either accept the underlying trend that most national politicians will deny but is staring us all in the face, namely, that our governments have become more and more centralised, and we should be honest enough to complete the process by funding local government entirely from the centre; or we should reverse this process and let local councils become different from each other, fully accountable to and almost exclusively financed by their local electorates.

The first route would mean that so long as the national tax receipts are gathered on a fair and equitable basis then personal objections to a slightly higher level of direct or indirect taxes, or a combination of both, would in time evaporate. I'm not saying it would be harmonious but it would become generally accepted, for it would mean the abolition of the Council Tax – crucially without replacement by any other tax. This could be achieved across the UK, for instance, by adding about 6p to income tax or increasing the VAT rate by 5%.[2] It would, of course, mean the end of local democracy, for without the ability to finance local deviations any semblance of independent action would disappear very quickly.

Some people are attracted to raising VAT as a means to abolishing local taxes altogether. It is a perfectly respectable position and far more rational and honest than the current financial smoke and mirrors. I believe, however, that it would result in a far more centralised state, placing our local councils in an economic, social and cultural straightjacket. Crucially, it would remove local accountability, as there would be little left to decide, making the election of councillors less important than it is now. It would undoubtedly reduce local diversity and colour – and for these three reasons should therefore be resisted.

To deliver ful accountability to local authorities will require a brave but realistic central government to do three things: firstly, to accept that postcode differences can be a good thing if the locals living in one area have voted to have different priorities from their neighbouring authority or the national norm: secondly, to remove those responsibilities better administered from the centre or directly by the consumers rather than give money to councils to administer them on the consumer's behalf; and, thirdly, to be prepared to reduce central government taxes so that the local taxes may rise to cover all or practically all of the locally-delivered services.

The clichéd criticism that the level of service in a local council area is a 'postcode lottery' has to be challenged. If we are to have local councils at all surely we must recognise that they can and should reflect the local demographic differences in population, the different topography, the often unique local traditions and history, the workforce, the skills, the natural resources, the relative wealth and so on? Local government should mean local differences, with accountability at a local level, while local administration of central services or entitlements should place the responsibility and accountability at a central government or parliamentary level. Understanding and defending such a separation then allows us to begin to unravel the mess that is local government, divesting it of responsibilities that it need not have.

As an example, consider if education were to be removed from the responsibility of local authorities. It could be delivered centrally, with each school being given a budget directly from the national education department on a per capita basis with additional grants and allowances for special educational services and capital expenditure. This is how schools have been run in New Zealand for the last eighteen years with successful results. Alternatively, schools could be funded by the equivalent of a voucher, or money-follows-pupil system, whereby a school receives funding from the state for every pupil it attracts. This is how schools are run in the Netherlands, again with great success. Neither of these approaches requires the administrative tier that, in Scotland, has local authority education departments using up £1.1 billion of expenditure before the education funding reaches the schools.[3] Not only could much of that money be saved; it would mean that the proportion of council spending that the current amount of Council Tax revenue would support would move from 16.7% to 25.9%. Move the centrally funded elderly care services to the NHS Boards and the proportion would change to 30.79%. Centrally fund the police and fire boards (the councillors could stay on them, but are hardly the guarantee of democratic accountability that they claim they are) and the proportion moves to 38.74%.[4]

Council Tax will never be able to pay for the whole of local government spending so what is required is to remove or significantly reduce the funding that comes from the centre for those responsibilities that local councils might retain and then to allow local authorities to raise the shortfall through taxes set by themselves. The reduction in transferring funds from the centre would allow a corresponding drop in central government taxes so that the difference to the consumer of the falling central taxes and rising local taxes would generally be neutral. In effect what we would be doing is recalibrating the local and national taxes so that where they are raised reflects where the real responsibility and accountability for delivering the service lies. This would establish true local accountability of a type that has not been seen since the advent of the welfare state at the end of the Second World War – a time when the Town Clerk was a highly respected position and Bailies were generally looked up to.

Local authorities can also be encouraged to charge consumers directly for some of their services so long as they remove that element from the Council Tax. For instance, we could learn from Ireland and allow councils to charge for refuse collection either as the service provider or as a regulator of private refuse collectors. Evidence from the Irish experience, where bins are charged on a pay-by-weight basis, suggests that even large families can reduce their costs because they become more environmentally aware and recycle and reduce their waste. Pensioners and single people who consume less can make significant savings.

My preference is for local government to raise the majority of the money it spends – just as the Scottish Parliament should. What is required first is the separation of all those public services that should be national in their funding, because they are currently being locally administered on behalf of central government. Then a broader tax base should be constructed so that the tax burden is spread over those that currently benefit from the services but make little contribution, as well as those that pay already.

Failure of the poll tax and Council Tax

It should be remembered that, after a thorough review of local government finances by the Conservatives in the 1980s, the poll tax was introduced to replace the widely unpopular domestic rates. Applied to Scotland a year early, against Margaret Thatcher's own better instincts, the poll tax was meant to ensure that everybody made some contribution towards the cost of local services in an attempt to make councils more accountable and responsive to local electors.

In the mythology, if not demonology, that has since followed the demise of the poll tax it is often forgotten that the tax was not a universal flat sum but included up to 80% relief for those on low incomes or in receipt of benefits or for those in certain employment groups such as nursing. These reliefs were not, however, tapered enough and, with some Labour councils forcing the tax to over £400 per head – when it was conceived and designed to be in the region of £250 – the poll tax became a byword for unfairness and injustice and its failure was sealed.

In its final year John Major's government raised VAT from 15% to 17.5% and used the additional 2.5% to fund local authorities and bring the poll tax down. This was to ensure that the new Council Tax was well received – after all, the Council Tax was just the unpopular domestic rates all over again except for the single occupant's discount and the banding of properties by their asset value rather than nominal rental value multiplied by a poundage (always an anachronism when the private rental market had all but disappeared).

I recall the night that the poll tax was abolished, 21 March 1991. I was live on BBC Scotland News with Christine Richard (then a Conservative councillor) and David Begg (then a Labour councillor) and I warned then that the new Council Tax would be a disaster, while my opponents welcomed it. The problem with Council Tax or indeed Local Income Tax is that so long as local taxes can be increased without a care for those that pay them then the problem of funding local government will continue to haunt us.

Initially, Council Tax was well received, but it was always my suspicion that it had more to do with the central government subsidy than a love of the tax system itself. Now, more than ten years on and with memories short and the subsidy's effect even shorter, all the pain that was once associated with domestic rates is now felt again with Council Tax.

Despite rebates available through Council Tax benefit, many older people point out the Council Tax's poor relationship with the ability to pay. The tax hits hardest those who have done the right thing and saved for their retirement. While property is easy to tax, because it does not move and is an asset that has an owner that can be pursued, its value does not necessarily reflect people's ability to pay and selling up and moving to a more modest property is not always possible or desirable. Those on fixed incomes, such as pensioners, can find continued Council Tax increases difficult to meet while next door neighbours with a number of earners will be paying less per head. Taxing disproportionately those who have planned for their retirement is a significant disincentive to save and for a country facing a pension black hole is especially daft.

If the Council Tax is the answer then it is clearly a rather stupid question, so let's start all over again.

A sales tax alternative

I have previously advocated the complete abolition of Council Tax and its replacement by a sales tax, partly out of devilment and the wish to provoke some debate about local government, and partly because of its merits of accountability, fairness and visibility.

The instincts of most British people will initially be negative, based, I suspect, upon a general suspicion of or dislike for the VAT system, although Britain's rate is below the European average and certainly lower than countries such as Denmark, where it is 25%.[5] Such instinctive opposition and possibly fear of high sales tax rates does not mean we should simply dismiss the idea. It can be shown that a sales tax does not have to be high, and that criticisms that it would be too complex or difficult are unfounded. Arguments that applying a sales tax in Scotland would be impractical can be countered by considering the US experience.

A study by the Institute of Fiscal Studies has shown that were the 20% of local authority spending that is funded by Council Tax to be raised through an increase in VAT then it would require an increase of about 5%. Now, go back to that original question and decide what local government is for and what it should do and the possibilities become more interesting. If the responsibilities of local authorities are significantly changed, such that the delivery of education or police no longer involves local councils and the amount of funding they are supplied with correspondingly drops, then the proportion of the tax raised to the money spent becomes much greater (thus increasing accountability) and there is the possibility of making marginal tax cuts. It might be possible to reduce the 5% down to 4% or even 3.5%.

Now take that 5% and add it to the goods and services that you buy, recognising that the necessities of life such as food and clothing are not taxed. Then one begins to see that people on fixed incomes could enjoy savings, while those that are consuming more, together with domestic and international tourists, who make no local contribution to local taxes, would be paying more. When considered this way, a sales tax becomes more attractive, certainly more so than the highly regressive Council Tax. Indeed the Office for National Statistics evidence shows that while VAT is regressive it is less so that Council Tax.[6]

A direct result of a sales tax system is tax competition, which is a distinct advantage over a property tax system such as Council Tax. At least the inevitability of the Council Tax's year-on-year rise would be challenged. This is for two reasons. To maximise revenues councils recognise that economic activity has to be encouraged – this doesn't always mean retail activity by the way, but can mean luxury tourism, for instance. Councils will suddenly have good reasons to attempt to fix a percentage that offers a competitive economic advantage against a neighbouring authority. If an authority does not want to cut its rate below its neighbour's it will still face pressure not to go above or risk the loss of income as shoppers make that extra effort to go to a bordering council's shopping mall.

The second point is that practically everybody contributes, adding a political incentive to keep taxes low. Too few of the electorate pay Council Tax and even fewer pay the whole amount without help of benefit. This reduces the numbers of taxpayers motivated to protest – sales tax is different and offers a clear advantage of accountability over Council Tax.

By letting local authorities vary a supplement on top of VAT, which would be collected at the point of a transaction and remitted back locally, we could have these advantages whilst restoring local accountability and variety.

Some critics of a sales tax argue that it would be too complex and too difficult. I don't accept this. Like VAT, a local sales tax would be easy to collect. Sales tax is used in countries across the world and we already have administrative systems collecting VAT. Revenue and Customs ensures that VAT is levied on all sales and this is paid over by the business on the customer's behalf. Unlike Council Tax,[7] or the poll tax,[8] collection levels are high as sales tax is difficult to avoid and penalties for non-compliance are severe on businesses.

The United States experience

In the United States both individual states and local municipalities use a local sales tax to everyone's purchases to finance state and county services. Amongst the smallest states there are seven with a population of less than a million, of which four levy a state sales tax and three do not. Those that levy a sales tax allow local municipalities to add their own levy within a band range. Alaska has no state sales tax but allows local sales taxes while Delaware and Montana have no sales tax at all.

Sales tax use in the USA's least populated states

State	Population	Pop.density (Sq Miles)	Taxable /Exempt	State Rate	Maximum local rate	Maximum total rate
Wyoming	509,294	5.25	T	4.00	2.00	6.00
Vermont	623,050	67.36	E	6.00	1.00	7.00
North Dakota	636,677	9.23	E	5.00	2.50	7.50
Alaska	663,661	1.16	T	None	7.00	7.00
South Dakota	775,933	10.23	T	4.00	2.00	6.00

[Source: US Federation Of Tax Administrators & US Census Bureau]

Populations between half a million to a million would be considered large for a local authority in Scotland (only Glasgow manages this distinction in Scotland) but, given that American states are broken into municipalities that can add their own levies, it can be seen that whether there is a high or low population, or even a high or low population density, is not a factor in the use of sales tax. Note that some states give exemptions for foods and some do not. I would not support any local sales tax differentiating from classifications used by VAT in the interests of simplicity and consumer understanding.

Alaska, the largest state in the United States, has 162 incorporated municipalities, made up of boroughs or cities, of which ninety levy a sales tax. Sales tax rates range from a low of 1% to a high of 7% and the 'typical' sales tax rates are from 3% to 5%. There are thirty-eight municipalities that levy a property tax, of which twenty-eight also have a sales tax.[8] In 2005 Alaskan local governments generated approximately $1.07 billion in revenues from property, sales and severance taxes, of which $858.4 million was from property taxes. There is no statewide sales tax levied and no personal state income tax in Alaska.

Although the Scottish island authorities are certainly small, they are larger than all but two of the ninety Alaskan municipalities that levy their own sales taxes, many of which are communities of less 5,000. Twenty of the thirty-two Scottish councils are over 100,000 and twenty-eight are over 75,000. Whilst it should be left to councils to determine the rate they might set their sales tax, councils would be free to pool the administration of collection were that to prove beneficial.

Experience in the USA is that sales taxes are levied at low rates and there is always pressure to keep the rate down. That same pressure could increase Scotland's public service efficiency and improve her economic competitiveness. It's not as if Council Tax is free from problems such as ability to pay. A sales tax meets the first criteria of the Council Tax protesters in that it relates more closely to people's ability to pay. In Hall and Smith's IFS report it was shown that the proportion of income paid by any citizen remains close to 3% – whether they are on a low or high income. The rich, in fact, pay a slightly greater proportion, as they are more likely to

Scottish local authorities ranked by population size

Ascending order

Orkney Islands	19,590
Shetland Islands	22,000
Eilean Siar	26,370
Clackmannanshire	48,630
Midlothian	79,190
Inverclyde	82,130
Stirling	86,930
Moray	88,120
East Renfrewshire	89,600
Argyll & Bute	90,870
West Dunbartonshire	91,400
East Lothian	91,800
East Dunbartonshire	105,960
Angus	109,170
Scottish Borders	109,730
South Ayrshire	111,780
East Ayrshire	119,400
North Ayrshire	135,830
Perth & Kinross	138,400
Dundee City	142,170
Dumfries & Galloway	148,340
Falkirk	149,150
West Lothian	163,780
Renfrewshire	170,000
Aberdeen City	202,370
Highland	213,590
Aberdeenshire	235,440
South Lanarkshire	306,280
North Lanarkshire	323,420
Fife	356,740
Edinburgh, City of	457,834
Glasgow City	578,790

[Source: General Register Office for Scotland]

spend on higher value items. Reflecting ability to pay requires some exemptions on necessities but that's already an accepted principle of the VAT system, as I've already mentioned.

Advantages of a sales tax

After reflecting ability to pay, the next major goal for any local taxation system is to bring greater accountability to local government. This was the *raison d'être* behind the Community Charge – everybody should pay something towards council services – but it was seen to fail on the ability to pay. In contrast, almost everyone would pay sales tax but it has the advantage of being fairer. There is a further advantage, which is that a sales tax is visible. Those who have experienced a sales tax in North America (it is also used extensively in Canada) will know that the till receipts are presented so that the pre-tax price is listed with the tax then shown and the total amount below. Some tills already operate like this in Britain – petrol receipts for instance. Such a visible tax system helps people become much more aware that they are paying for local authority services and would highlight their right to say what the quality and level of service should be. Councillors would be more likely to be elected in line with local people's wishes and become accountable, providing value for money. We might even see increases in the numbers of people voting at council elections if people were directly affected by the result. Examples from the USA are compelling. As the Independence Institute notes: 'Local tax competition gives Colorado citizens choices in where they shop, live, and work. . . Tax competition is not a dirty word, it means that at the local level taxpayers are able to get the government they desire and are willing to pay for.'[9]

Tax competition already works for UK citizens in the south of England who travel to France on 'booze cruises' to beat the UK's swingeing excise duties on alcohol – and it has existed for many years on the border between the Republic of Ireland and Northern Ireland for petrol and cigarettes. Such human behaviour would soon be replicated between Edinburgh and West Lothian or Glasgow and Renfrew.

There are also other economic benefits for a country like

Scotland. At present, our cities are penalised because business rates do not accrue to the authorities where the payments originate but are redistributed to rural areas and dormitory towns where far fewer businesses exist. With a local sales tax urban councils could make up this loss, thus allowing them to pay for the many additional burdens their businesses, tourists and the needs of commuters generate. Replace Council Tax with a sales tax and economic growth is encouraged and rewarded – suddenly the workers and visitors alike are contributing to a city's industriousness and the city's finances can begin to meet the heavy demands they face.

So, assuming current rates of spending, what would all this cost us? The IFS estimated that a transfer of Council Tax to sales tax in the UK would mean a rate of 4.5%. This would be slightly higher in Scotland (5%), due to our lower level of economic activity compared with the UK as a whole, but comparable to most US states, where the average is at the upper end of a zero to 7% range. Local sales tax and VAT would then total about 22.5%, depending on how councils saw their need for spending. Although high in UK terms, it would not be out of the ordinary for Europe, with the EU member average standing at almost 20% in 2003, and the highest at 25%.

It's undoubtedly time we properly reformed our system of local taxation in Scotland. A local sales tax would more closely reflect the ability to pay and would broaden the taxpayer base, ensuring increased accountability. With rates likely to be comparable to the USA and Canada, the tax should gain broad acceptance. Sales tax also has the benefits that it is easy to collect and will bring tax competition between councils. This creates a permanent downward pressure on rates to ensure value for money for local taxpayers. The radical solution we seek has proven its merit in North America and would create a virtuous tax regime for Scottish councils.

No single tax can deliver enough revenue without hurting one group or another while achieving the goal of making local councils self-financing and truly local. I am, therefore, willing to concede that a basket of a number of taxes shall have to be found so that the tax base is broad enough and the rates are relatively low. The sales tax must, however, be seen as a serious contender for inclusion in such a local fiscal formula as it is one of the few taxes where there is an imperative is to keep the rate low.

NOTES

1. Scottish Local Government Financial Statistics 2004–05; £1.614 billion raised in Council Tax (13.7% of revenue) and a further £344 million received in Council Tax rebate from Treasury (2.9%) giving a total of 16.6% of revenue or 16.7% of expenditure.
2. John Hall and Stephen Smith: *Local Sales Taxation*, Institute of Fiscal Studies, London, 1995.
3. Research by Colin Robertson of the Scottish Conservative Research Department established that in 2002–03 there was a gap of £1.1 billion between total schools expenditure and budgeted schools running costs – money held back and spent by local authorities.
4. Scottish Local Government Financial Statistics 2004–05.
5. _____

EU states with standard VAT rates higher than the UK's 17.5%

Denmark	25.0%	Austria	20.0%	Hungary	19.0%
Sweden	25.0%	Hungary	20.0%	Netherlands	19.0%
Finland	22.0%	Italy	20.0%	Slovakia	19.0%
Poland	22.0%	Slovenia	20.0%	Estonia	18.0%
Portugal	22.0%	France	19.6%	Latvia	18.0%
Belgium	21.0%	Czech	19.0%	Lithuania	18.0%
Ireland	21.0%	Greece	19.0%	Malta	18.0%

Only four – Germany, Spain, Cyprus and Luxembourg – have VAT rates lower than the UK.

[Source Official EU figures]

6. Jones, Francis, The effects of taxes and benefits on household income, 2004/05; Office for National Statistics.
7. Council Tax collection rates for Scotland were as low as 88.3% in 1999–2000 rising year-on-year to reach 92.7% in 2004–05. The English collection rate has risen from 95.6% to 96.1% in the same period (Scottish Executive figures).
8. £637 million of poll tax remained uncollected in March 2000; Parliamentary Question by Bill Aitken MSP, 1 March 2000.
9. Other types of local taxes levied in Alaska are raw fish taxes, 'bed' taxes in hotels, severance taxes, liquor and tobacco taxes, gaming (pull tabs) taxes and fuel transfer taxes.
10. Barry Poulson: *Local Tax Competition is Great*, Independence Institute, Golden, Colorado, 16 May 2001.

Chapter 7

LET DEATH DUTIES DIE

'What is the difference between a taxidermist and a tax collector? The taxidermist takes only your skin.'
— MARK TWAIN

Inheritance tax is highly corrosive. All your life you have worked hard, paid your taxes and put a little aside for that rainy day. You have always wanted to give your children or grandchildren a better start in life than your parents were able to give you. I firmly believe it is these natural family instincts that keep us moving forward in a socially cohesive manner, binding us together and making our communities a warm supportive place to be. Blood *is* thicker than water and it is this familial blood that courses through the veins and feeds the minds of parents, aunts, uncles and grandparents when they make economic decisions.

But there's a catch. With 67% of housing now owned privately[1] and with a large growth in property values a large majority of Scots are finding that rather than letting them leave a nice nest egg to their offspring the taxman is taking a rather large slice.

Since Gordon Brown became Chancellor the threshold at which

inheritance tax is paid has hardly changed at all – moving from £210,000 in 1997 to only £285,000 in 2006.[2] Meanwhile, property prices have gone through the roof, increasing 187% in ten years.[3] The result is that the estates of one million more people are falling liable to tax. With the growth in living standards and property values since the 1980s, inheritance tax (IHT) is now a significant revenue generator for the UK government, at around £2.5 billion in 2001. With such a growth – expected to be £3.3 billion in 2006[4] – there is a real concern, already voiced by the Forsyth Tax Commission report,[5] that if IHT is not reformed soon it will become too expensive to tackle.

Inheritance tax was first introduced as a tax on estates in 1796. Unsurprisingly, the value changed over time and the scope of estate duty was extended. Influential arguments in favour of estate duties were put forward by Thomas Paine and Alexis de Toqueville, with their roots in the dislike, if not hatred, of the European aristocracy. In America it was thought that taxing inheritance would avoid the curse of the idle rich that resulted in a dangerous and anti-democratic concentration of power and dampening of economic endeavour in Europe. In two works, *The Rights of Man* (1791) and *Agrarian Justice* (1797), Paine argued for the adoption of an inheritance tax in England to balance out the unfair distribution of 'landed property'. By 1857 estates worth over £20 were taxable but duty was rarely collected on estates valued under £1500.

David Lloyd George said that 'Death is the ideal time to tax rich people' and that 'all inherited wealth is unearned by its nature'. His views were built on the belief that property rights could be violated and wealth transferred from one group to another. The argument goes – and has not just been put by socialists but by Milton Friedman – that inheritance taxes do not impact on the economy. In an entirely individualist world, where parents and grandparents would have no care to establish family wealth and establish dynasties, that might be true, but such a world does not exist, as the establishment of family trusts and the transference of company ownership down family lines, all of which continue, to this day, surely evidence.

In his People's Budget of 1909 David Lloyd George increased Death Duties by more than 50% so that they would raise

£4.4 million a year, a large amount considering that tobacco and spirits duties were planned to deliver £3.5 million in the same year.[6] The argument in favour of this increase was fuelled by the envy of others and hung on the slogan of transferring the wealth of the undeserving rich to the deserving poor. Estate duty was replaced in 1975 by Capital Transfer Tax, which was replaced by inheritance tax (IHT) in 1986. Currently, in the UK, a surviving spouse pays nothing. All other bequests above £263,000 are subject to taxation at 40% as of March 1987. Prior to this date there were a number of tiered rates. The estate of a deceased person includes all of their worldly belongings, including houses and other property from caravans to yachts to stamp collections and works of art. On death there is a six-month limit to pay inheritance tax, during which solicitors assess the value of the estate and consider challenges. If there is insufficient cash to pay the tax and the solicitors' bill, then assets must be sold.[7]

'Inheritance tax used to be a problem for the rich. Now it's a problem for you and me', says Anne Young, a tax expert at Scottish Widows, who calculates that about 1 in 3 of Britain's 24 million households now have estates that would fall within the taxman's reach.[8]

Everyone should be concerned. One only needs to look at the property pages for one's neighbourhood to recognise that it is no longer difficult for a moderate property to make what would not be considered especially wealthy people liable to the inheritance tax. Do people who live in properties valued over £285,000 in Scotland consider themselves part of the landed gentry or wealthy aristocracy that the tax was originally conceived to soak?[9]

It is not as if we have never paid taxes whilst alive. This is a double taxation for all and a treble taxation for some. People pay their income tax on their earnings and then after that tax deduction pay VAT on their spending (not to mention the Council Tax too) so some of the assets captured by IHT have come from taxed income spent on taxed goods. A treble whammy. Likewise, if you invest your money you pay tax on the interest and it becomes a taxable asset again on death. Why should the wealth we worked so hard to create be taxed again on our death, for the second or third time, simply because we wish to pass it on to our friends or family?

In a society which sees the family under assault should we not be encouraging giving to our relations? Why should acts of kindness be taxed like this – do we not want a more giving, more caring society?

Of course the people that the tax was aimed at – originally the aristocracy and then latterly the nouveau riche – can afford expensive tax lawyers and will put their money in complicated trusts or move to Monaco and exotic islands where their wealth can't be reached. But this approach is not so easy if you live in Glebe Street, Auchtermuchty. More ordinary routes to avoidance currently include: the giving of money in a trust fund before death; the giving of money seven years before death (subject to a maximum before tax applies of some £5,000 a year); transferring assets to a spouse; and, generally, gifts made seven years before death – all exempt from inheritance tax.

Consider, also, how many of our finest buildings, now ruined and dilapidated, would still have occupants with the money to make sure their architectural splendours were there for all to see, instead of being a drain on a public purse that cannot afford to restore them? How many glorious works of art would still be hung on British walls available for public view instead of being sold to foreign galleries and museums to pay for this insidious tax?

In 2005 the then Tory leader Michael Howard considered but never committed to offering relief to those people now faced with this new tax through no fault of their own. The idea originally floated was to raise the tax threshold to, say, one million pounds, which would have reduced the tax take to just £300 million.[10] There comes a point, however, when a tax becomes uneconomic to collect and the solution is to abolish it.

One doesn't have to be a Conservative sympathiser to advocate this position; there are supporters of low tax liberal economics in even the Labour Party and the appeal for a more meritocratic society makes abolishing inheritance tax especially attractive to such people. Debate over inheritance tax has been raised by former Labour Chief Secretary to the Treasury, Stephen Byers, who called for inheritance tax to be abolished, arguing that it was now hurting middle-class homeowners, including those in marginal electoral constituencies.[11] Byers also argued that the tax is unfair because the very wealthy tend to get advice on how to avoid paying it, but 'this is not an option if your only asset of any real worth is the family home'. Supporters of Gordon Brown quickly counterattacked[12], pointing out that inheritance tax brings in about £3 billion in revenue annually and depicting it as a levy on a small elite. But the future trend for inheritance tax is towards considerable growth in the number of families affected by it.

There are two reasons for this. Firstly, the tax is currently levied on about 5% of the estates of people who die.[13] But that percentage will change dramatically in the next fifteen years as the baby-boomer generation starts to die off and pass its property and other assets on. Halifax Financial Services calculates that property worth £340 billion will change hands between now and 2020 – about 10% of the total housing stock in the UK and the largest transfer of housing wealth in British history. The impact is so big because the baby boomers have transformed home ownership: in Britain almost 70% of households now own their own homes, more than double the 31% that did in 1946. Secondly, Halifax calculates that the IHT threshold of £285,000 would now be £390,000 if it had been increased in line with the 187% increase in house prices over the past ten years and that the number of homes worth more than the threshold has risen by 72% in the past five years, standing at an estimated 2.4 million – a fourfold increase since 1994 – and will rise to 4 million in 2015 and 6 million in 2025 if the threshold is not raised in 'real' terms. 'The threshold needs to reflect what happened in the property market,' says Tim Crawford, group economist at HBOS. A survey conducted by NOP found that 71% of people in the UK think that the current threshold level for IHT is unfair and 65% believe that the government should adjust the IHT threshold in line with house-price inflation.

Practice elsewhere

Countries such as Germany, France, Belgium the Netherlands and Switzerland have taxes on beneficiaries. In Germany *Erbschaftsteue* is paid by the beneficiary: spouses pay 7% on legacies above £187,000, rising to 30% on legacies above £15.75 million on a sliding scale. Non-spouse relatives and non-relatives pay marginally higher sliding scales on the legacies they receive. In France, *droits de succession* are also paid by the beneficiary. The tax is levied in theory from the first euro passed on, but a series of tax-free thresholds apply to family members, including $50,000 for children of the deceased. A surviving spouse pays 5% on legacies above £46,000, rising on a sliding scale to 40% on legacies above £1.081 million. Other relatives pay at similar rates but with lower tax-free allowances. This means that the value of even a modest two-bedroom apartment in central Paris is enough to push families into a 30% tax bracket. For non-family members and unmarried partners, the situation is even more complicated, with inheritance tax rising as high as 60%, with nearly no tax-free allowance. In October 2003, a group of French Deputies from President Chirac's centre-right party proposed a parliamentary resolution to abolish inheritance tax altogether. It failed. Another initiative in 2005 to exclude principal residences from the tax suffered the same fate, but it is believed that the Finance Ministry is considering plans to suppress *droits de succession* between spouses in the 2007 budget.

In Spain spouses have to pay 8.5% on legacies above £11,000, rising to 34% on legacies above £542,300, with a complex exemption system that depends on the length of time *post mortem* that the beneficiary keeps the assets. When the surviving spouse dies, inheritance tax has to be paid again – but this time on 100% rather than 50% of the assets. Switzerland has no *erbschaftssteuer* at national level. However, in the various cantons, three possibilities (a tax on the estate, a tax on the beneficiaries, or no tax) exist.

In the USA, a surviving spouse pays nothing. All other bequests above £765,000 are subject to federal taxation at 45%, with additional local taxes pushing that figure above 50% in many states. When the current republican administration came into office in January 2001, the lower threshold was only £344,000; it has more than doubled in just 5 years. Since 2002, the top rate has been 50%, and under current legislation this will decrease to 0% in 2010, and rebound back to 50% in 2011. Cynics might ask if there will be an increase in deaths in 2010 as a consequence! Some States, such as New Mexico, South Dakota, South Carolina and Utah, have abolished their own taxes so that only the federal tax is levied.

Japan had one of the highest inheritance taxes of Western economies: in 2003 it dropped from an infamous 70% down to 50% and is only levied on Japanese holding Japanese assets. While that still seems high, in fact with all the various deductions that can be claimed the actual rate is more like 30%. When the government dropped the gift tax rate back in 2003 to allow those over 65 to make a one-time gift of 25 million yen per child, the resultant deluge of cash pumped 1 trillion yen into the economy in that year alone.

The Japanese experience is not unique. In Australia the changes to inheritance tax in Queensland caused a reaction across the whole country – a scenario that could be replicated in Europe or within the United Kingdom. In 1977 the premier of Queensland, Sir John Bjelke-Person, eliminated the tax, partly to encourage business people and others to move to that state. The then Liberal Prime Minister, Malcolm Fraser, endorsed the action and abolished Federal Estate Tax in 1978 as well. The effect was dramatic: with other states fearing emigration and hence capital flight they followed suit and abolished theirs as well. The resultant fear of tax competition spread the abolitionist approach across Australia. By 1984 all estate duties (including gifts) had been removed, both state and federal, despite various tax review committees recommending refinements to improve the equity, efficiency and simplicity of the tax. The subsequent rapid rise in population in the Gold Coast, Brisbane and the Sunshine Coast led to a building boom that has lasted for three decades.

In Italy the inheritance tax was abolished as part of a drive against bureaucracy, the winning argument being that tax administration could be utilised more productively elsewhere. The Prodi election campaign in 2006 promised to reinstate inheritance tax but it has not yet become a reality.

Other countries have their own quite disparate reasons for not having an inheritance tax. Sweden eliminated its tax because a wealth tax of 1.5% each year made it redundant and was able to raise significantly more revenue. Canada has not had an inheritance tax since it was repealed by Brian Mulroney's government in the 1980s. Instead it now taxes realised capital gains at death – amounting to a *de facto* form of inheritance tax.

What do you do in a Communist country attempting to spread

wealth through dynamic economic growth? Well, you probably don't want an inheritance tax (where of course it previously was not needed). In China there is little sign of future imposition due to concerns that it will punish up-and-coming entrepreneurs. A survey[14] found that 68.4% of people did not believe that the inheritance tax would appropriately adjust income disparity and a perceptive 56.5% said the general public might suffer great economic loss as a result, rather than the extremely wealthy targeted.

Targeting the wealthy?

Writing in *The Independent*,[15] Johann Hari has argued: 'Most people can tolerate Bill Gates or Richard Branson, because they can see that they have done something to earn their vast wealth. Yet they feel queasy when they look at James Murdoch and the Duke of Westminster, who seem to be rich because of who their fathers are, not because of their own abilities.' The attack may appeal to atavistic emotions, but is of course as redundant as Lloyd George's appeal to tax the dead rich when one realises that the rich have employed tax accountants and advisors to ensure that very little if any of their millions go to the taxpayer.

   Andrew Carnegie was another vocal supporter of a federal inheritance tax in America. In his book *The Gospel of Wealth* (1889) Carnegie cited three ways for a wealthy man to dispose of his accumulated riches. Leaving it to one's family he hated; donating it for public use he was willing to put up with, although it was an abdication of duty; for he wanted to encourage the third, the philanthropy of wealthy men while alive. Carnegie asked the question: 'Why should men leave great fortunes to their children?' and answered himself: 'great sums bequeathed often work more for the injury than the good of the recipients'. Carnegie supported inheritance tax not so much because it created finance for good public deeds but because of the unintended consequence of encouraging wealthy men to become philanthropists when they were alive. Carnegie ends his book by saying: 'The man who dies rich dies disgraced', and he was true to his word, giving away 90% of his wealth in his own lifetime.

Others in America, such as Teddy Roosevelt in the past (at the same time as Andrew Carnegie) and now billionaire Warren Buffet or the father of Bill Gates, William Gates Snr, have all argued that inherited wealth is essentially unfair.

My answer to these points is that they may in some, even the majority, of instances be true. Yes, it may seem unfair for some people to receive riches without having to work for it – although a family may have been instrumental in helping to accumulate that wealth. Yes, the imposition of an inheritance tax may act as an incentive for great philanthropy – although it should be noted that such a tax was not needed to encourage Carnegie himself and that his argument was put before the introduction of higher personal tax rates and the comprehensive reach of the welfare state that together have discouraged philanthropy for a variety of predictable reasons. Yes, the easy gain of inherited wealth and the living off it may dampen entrepreneurial spirit – although I've never heard it said that the business birth rate is lower in Scotland than in England because of the great inherited wealth of the idle rich in the former. Yes, it may be that the establishment of new or the survival of old aristocracies may lead to a concentration of power – although the previous argument about the somnambulism and fecklessness of the undeserving wealthy would suggest such dynasties would not necessarily survive for long and indeed it is not difficult to find evidence of such self-inflicted collapse.

For me, however, it is not that each of these arguments can in fact be challenged successfully that matters; it is that they all stem from the central belief that society can and should be engineered, and that the state should have the authority to conduct its fiscal policies to produce a particular social outcome even if that requires the confiscation of property legally obtained. Yet, even if one believes that the social engineers have the better of the argument, both the predictable outcomes – such as the rich being able to afford to avoid inheritance tax – and the unintended consequences – such as the shifting relationship between property values and tax thresholds ensuring that more and more relatively modest families have become liable for the tax, and the break up of great cultural collections and loss of architectural gems – must surely convince many that the tax is not worth continuing with?

Abolishing inheritance tax in Scotland

The revenue gathered from inheritance tax in Scotland is currently £140 million (see table) and rising, though still less than 6% of the UK total[16.] If the Scottish Parliament were to have IHT included in any fiscal autonomy settlement it would be one of my priorities for abolition. Here is why. Firstly, at £140 million it is a relatively cheap tax to abolish and, secondly, it will quickly begin to pay for itself because it would make Scotland a place for successful entrepreneurs to locate to.

Scottish revenue from inheritance tax

Year	Scotland (£ million)	United Kingdom (£ million)	Scottish % share
2000–01	100	2,200	4.54
2001–02	170	2,357	7.21
2002–03	140	2,356	5.94
2003–04	140	2,504	5.59

[Source: SPICe December 2006]

The abolition of inheritance tax in Scotland would not only remove a burden which penalises modest families, undermines the work ethic and is built upon the cancer of envy, it would make Scotland a place for wealthy people to come and live, play and spend their money. They wouldn't have to die in Scotland, just have our wee country as their tax jurisdiction. Their demand for high standards would help us raise the quality of our goods and services and, as an example, our tourism industry would find competition driving it to ever higher quality. As in Australia, the result might even be that tax competition from Scotland in inheritance taxes would drive the Treasury in London to do the same.

NOTES

1. Scotland's housing is 67% privately owned and 7% privately rented.
2. Wright Hassall Solicitors, 'Inheritance Tax Fact Sheet', 2006.
3. Average house prices across the UK were £62,453 in the first quarter of 1996, compared to £179,425 as they stand in the third quarter of 2006, a rise of 187% over the past ten years. The average house price now equates to 62% of the IHT threshold compared with 42% ten years ago, according to Halifax, article viewable on www.aboutproperty.co.uk.
4. The revenue raised by the government through IHT has risen by £1bn since 1995/96 from £1.5 billion to £2.5 billion in 2003/04. A further 16% rise was estimated for 2004/05 to £2.9 billion followed by a projected increase to £3.3 billion in 2005/06 (14%). This would represent a more than doubling since 1996/97. Inland Revenue, HMT Pre-Budget Report, December 2004.
5. Michael Forsyth (Chairman): *Tax Matters, Reforming the Tax System*, Report of the Tax Reform Commission, London, 2006.
6. BBC.
7. Thomson Snell & Passmore, May 2006.
8. As cited in Peter Grumbel: 'Death's other Sting', *Time Europe Magazine*, 27 August 2006.
9. All the savings and assets have to be added in to the calculation too, so being below the threshold is no guarantee that an estate will not be subject to tax.
10. Estates valued at under £1,000,000 accounted for 90% of all estates paying IHT and 54% of all IHT revenue raised in 2001/02 (latest available figures).
11. Stephen Byers: 'Labour's next PM must abolish inheritance tax', *Sunday Telegraph*, 20 August 2006.
12. Will Woodard: 'Brown allies slap down ex-minister's call to scrap inheritance tax', *The Guardian*, 21 August 2006.
13. Around 5% of estates are estimated to pay IHT this year (32,000). The number has more than doubled since 1996/97 (15,000). Inland Revenue, HMT Pre-Budget Report, December 2004.
14. Social Investigation Centre from China Youth Daily and the News Centre from Tencent Company.
15. Johann Hari, *The Independent*, 3 December 2006.
16. About 40% of taxpayers, accounting for half of IHT revenues, reside in London and the South East, according to two special exercises carried out by the Inland Revenue. (Regional figures are not normally available.)

Conclusion

RISING TO THE CHALLENGE

'There is no such thing as a good tax.'
– WINSTON CHURCHILL

If localism is good – and I say it is, because it means councils being responsive and accountable to local taxpayers – then it must also mean the Scottish Parliament, the Welsh and Northern Ireland assemblies being accountable to their national taxpayers. The current level of structural economic subsidies must, over, say, the length of two parliaments, be phased out and the local institutions must raise, either directly or through the assignation of taxes gathered in their fiefdoms, far more – or even all – of the money that they spend. Politicians who feel the pain of taxpayers think twice before making more demands on the public purse; they learn to prioritise and become self-disciplined.

Every passing day that this policy is resisted makes Scotland more dependent upon England – and paradoxically at greater risk from separation from the United Kingdom.

For a free-market liberal like myself, such goals as reducing public spending and taxes are relatively tame, but their goals are undoubtedly radical and shocking to many in collectivist Scotland –

even most Conservative politicians recoil, lest it frighten the horses.
If there were to be a proper debate in Scotland about the limits of
government and what it should do then the suggestions I have made
are rather modest and limited. Arthur Seldon, writing in 'Corrigible
Capitalism, Incorrigible Socialism'[1], provides a rough rule of
thumb that illustrates how far behind in economic and political
thought Scotland is becoming:

> Government should largely confine itself to 'public goods' – defence,
> law and order, environmental protection and other activities that
> require finance by taxation because their benefits cannot be refused
> to people who refuse to pay in prices. The remainder is best left to
> private enterprise to finance by charging. The dividing line between
> public and private goods is not always sharply defined; a practical
> working rule-of-thumb is: tax where you must (because pricing is
> impracticable); charge where you can. This rule yields approximate
> results, a kind of rough justice. But contrasted with the deficiencies,
> inflexibility and corruption of government in state economy it scores
> very high. Of that the history of the West since the industrial
> revolution and especially since the 1939–45 war, leaves no doubt.

While Scotland was, to its own benefit, forced to take on board
small government thinking during some of the eighteen years of
Conservative government between 1979 and 1997, it has been able
to ignore it since 1997 and turn its back on it altogether since 1999.
This was of course the goal of the many Socialists who wanted
what they considered to be 'Thatcherism' to stop at Hadrian's
Wall. Meanwhile, as the Index on Freedom[2] so ably reports, the
world, especially Eastern Europe, has been moving on and leaving
Scotland behind. Globalisation is not just about the new markets
that are opening up in goods and services, driving down prices and
relieving poverty[3]; it is also about the tax competition between
provinces and states that is driving down corporate and personal
tax rates so that economies can grow through innovation,
productivity and adaptability, all of this supporting a rise in
standards of living, especially for the poorest.

While the Baltic states, Russia and much of central Europe,
including Slovakia and Romania, are leaving no stone unturned to

make their economies dynamic and attractive enough to retain their best minds and hardest workers – despite all the seduction of the more developed countries of the West – Scotland continues to operate as if the Cold War still existed and the old style of mixed economy were the desirable model.[4]

Sadly, this lack of awareness to what is happening in the real economic world, even on our doorstep in Ireland, Iceland and Eastern Europe, suggests to me that Scotland will not change until there is an economic shock that forces us to do so. This worries me greatly[5] for there is no certainty that the causes of such a shock would not easily be misdiagnosed and the blame put on institutions such as our union with the rest of the United Kingdom. This would certainly suit the nationalists.

To open up Scotland to the low tax, low regulation, small government competition that it faces in the future requires the current collectivist consensus to be destroyed. It requires brave politicians from all parties to turn their backs on yet more legislation that interferes with our personal lives and inhibits our economic growth. There is a job to be done by the media, by academics and by think tanks, but until the principle is conceded that our Scottish state is already too big we will continue to hurtle towards competition with other countries that are no longer disadvantaged by 'enjoying' more Socialism than we do.

The next four years should begin by the Scottish Parliament starting to review the legislation that has already been passed, to determine what is working, what is failing and what would be better repealed and left to the voluntary actions of people and institutions. 'Holyrood repeals one of its own laws' really would be a front-page shock, horror, probe story.

It then needs a Scottish Executive to bring forward proposals for greater scrutiny of public spending at every stage, from its own budgeting, its financial memorandum for bills (including amended stages), through to more focus on post-legislative scrutiny and greater resourcing of subject committees so that they can better scrutinise the financial statements of departments. While all of these are the prerogative of the Parliament, in reality it requires the Scottish Executive to initiate such reforms or they will fail to gain the majority support they require.

The Scottish Executive must create a Treasury Department that not only deals with all of the tasks of the current Finance Department but actually becomes the gatekeeper of public finances, holding greater influence over the spending of departments, gathering more disaggregated financial information about Scotland and preparing for the collection of revenues of Scottish taxes and the negotiations that will in future be required with the UK Treasury over the reform of the Barnett Formula and the arrival of fiscal autonomy.

The first speech of the First Minister should include an announcement that business rates will be cut for all businesses by 12.5% below the Uniform Business Rate, with planned cuts of a further 12.5% for each of the remaining three years of that parliament.

It should also announce that there will be no growth in public spending over that period and that efficiency gains will be used to reduce taxation levels, initially of business and then personal incomes, with the intention of achieving reserves by the end of the second year that would allow a Tartan Tax cut of 3p in the third year of the Parliament.

In his or her first speech the finance minister should announce that he or she will be seeking discussions with the Chancellor of the Exchequer for the introduction of a standard rate cut of 3p, how that will be managed (see table below) and what arrangements can be made for the accrual to Scotland of tax revenues due to any improved productivity and increased consumption.

Cost of tax cuts over four years (£ million)[6]

Tax Cut	Year 1	Year 2	Year 3	Year 4
Tartan Tax cost	0	200	870	0
Business Rates cost	241	241	241	241
Annual cost	241	441	1111	241
Cumulative cost	241	682	1793	2034

Similar announcements should be made regarding discussions with the Treasury about what arrangements can be put in place for the Scottish Parliament becoming self-financing within the Union, so that full parliamentary scrutiny and debate can be allowed before proposals can be put to the Scottish electorate by the next Parliamentary elections in 2011.

For local government we require the same process of establishing as close as self-sufficiency as is possible. This will require the political parties that form the Scottish Executive to bring forward ways of delivering those local services – such as education – directly through schools or clusters of schools that do not require councils to distribute money or administer them.

Beyond 2011, or whenever fiscal autonomy is possible, the options to radically alter the economic incentives and the economic culture of Scotland become far greater. The introduction of a sales tax as a component of a basket of local taxes for local authorities – which could be left to local authorities to initiate – would be one of my priorities. The other would be to abolish the inheritance tax in Scotland.

In the meantime unionists should be very careful not to defend the Union on the basis of a 'Union Dividend' that is always going to provide a subsidy to Scotland. The Union can provide an insurance against times that are hard, but there are premiums to be paid and unionists should be comfortable with advocating payments towards the general UK pot that helps poorer regions or nations of the United Kingdom in times of hardship. Scotland should be aiming to be the workshop and the driver of the Union again, even if it is done not by building ships or locomotives or mining coal but by selling financial services or providing creative and cultural intellectual property.

Only if Scotland takes the lead within the Union in cutting taxes and reigning back spending so that its people will choose to stay and build the country rather than migrate south to London or further afield can we reverse the relative economic decline that we are experiencing and which is likely to accelerate in the face of competition. It is a massive challenge, but it is nothing compared to what Scotland achieved in its first three hundred years within the Union. If Scotland does not rise to this challenge now, I fear it will be faced with the harder task of doing it alone and outside the United Kingdom.

NOTES

1. Arthur Seldon: 'Corrigible Capitalism, Incorrigible Socialism', from *The Virtues of Capitalism*, The Collected Works of Arthur Seldon, Indianapolis: Liberty Fund, Indianapolis, 2004.

2. Marc A. Miles, Kim R. Holmes and Mary Anastasia O'Grady: *2006 Index of Economic Freedom*, The Heritage Foundation, Washington DC and The Wall Street Journal, New York, 2006.

3. There is no greater exponent of the benefits of globalisation, deregulation, low taxes and open societies under the rule of law than Deepak Lal's recent book. See Deepak Lal: *Reviving the Invisible Hand*, Princeton University Press, Princeton, 2006.

4. By 'old style' I mean the 1970s British economy when the state owned Associated British Ports, British Aerospace, British Leyland, British Airways, British Steel, British Coal, British Telecom (within The Post Office), Amersham International, Enterprise Oil, Sealink, Jaguar, Britoil, British Petroleum, British Gas, British Railways and the electricity industry. Looking around me in the Scottish Parliament there is hardly anybody that, had they been politicians in the 1980s, would have supported any of those privatisations that have so changed our country's prosperity.

5. Most likely an unwillingness to recognise that we are spending more than we earn and behaving as if the world owes us a living.

6. The cost of tax cuts in the first year includes the setting up of the administration which has been priced at the worse case scenario of £200 million, although it may be as low as only £20 million. The table shows the cumulative cost which are the amounts that spending would have to be reduced through savings against projections for those years. Given that various efficiency gains and savings range about £750–£3,000 million, the prospect of finding a total saving of £2,034 million within four years appears eminently achievable.